HOW TO
PAY FOR
COLLEGE

HOW TO
PAY FOR
COLLEGE

A Library How-To Handbook

Editors of the
American Library Association

Skyhorse Publishing

Skyhorse Publishing books may be purchased in bulk at special discounts for sales promotion, corporate gifts, fund-raising, or educational purposes. Special editions can also be created to specifications. For details, contact the Special Sales Department, Skyhorse Publishing, 307 West 36th Street, 11th Floor, New York, NY 10018 or info@skyhorsepublishing.com.

Skyhorse® and Skyhorse Publishing® are registered trademarks of Skyhorse Publishing, Inc.®, a Delaware corporation.

www.skyhorsepublishing.com

10 9 8 7 6 5 4 3 2 1

Library of Congress Cataloging-in-Publication Data

How to pay for college : a library how-to handbook / by editors of the American Library Association.
     p. cm.
 Includes bibliographical references and index.
 ISBN 978-1-61608-155-3 (pbk. : alk. paper)
 1. College costs--United States. 2. Education--United States--Finance. 3. Scholarships--United States. 4. Student aid--United States. I. American Library Association.
 LB2342.H575 2011
 378.3--dc22

                          2010047768

ALA ISBN: 978-0-8389-1077-1

Printed in China

Contents

"Beyond the Books" in Today's Public Libraries

Are you aware of all the resources that your public library offers "beyond the books"? Today's community libraries offer a lot more than books, audiobooks, and movies to check out. You can attend a free workshop or lecture, browse online resources that aren't available anywhere else, and use your library's computers and software programs to prepare for a test or master a new skill—all for free.

CHECK IT OUT!

You probably used public library resources as a grade-schooler and are familiar with the basics of locating a specific book or magazine. (If you're not, ask a librarian for help—you'll relearn this very quickly!) But you should also be aware of these basics offered by any public library today:

Interlibrary loan: If your library doesn't have the book or resource you want, you may be able to borrow it from another branch or library system through interlibrary loan. It's easy to use, and you can pick up your requested materials at your local library.

Reference section: Generally, reference materials are not available for checkout, but you can browse, read, and photocopy them in the library. *The Ultimate Scholarship Guide 2010* is a good example.

Computer stations: Your library may require that you reserve a computer, that you limit your time to a half hour or an hour at a time, or that you use certain computers for certain tasks. (Some libraries have computers dedicated to homework or to job searches.) Check the rules before you sit down.

Internet access: Your library is likely to offer wireless Internet access in addition to computer stations. In this case, you can bring your laptop computer (or see if library laptops are available for checkout), find a comfortable seat, and surf the college sites for free.

Subscription databases: You'll read about databases in this book that can give your search a boost. Public and school libraries have paid subscriptions to comprehensive online databases of college search information that simply aren't available anywhere else.

Specialty librarians: Depending on the size of your library system, librarians specializing in jobs and careers may be available in your local branch or elsewhere within the library system.

Classes, workshops, programs: Public libraries routinely offer free classes, tutorials, workshops, and other educational programs. College search topics may include choosing the right college for you, applying to colleges online, writing the college application essay, and more.

LIBRARIES AND POTENTIAL COLLEGE STUDENTS

Part of the mission of any public library is to meet the needs of its community. So, beyond stocking resources to help students with schoolwork, providing books, magazines, and newspapers for entertainment and information, and offering Internet access to the public, your library probably offers workshops and seminars to help students figure out how to pay for college. How much it offers will depend on the library's budget, available resources, and innovation.

Find out what your local library is doing—no matter how scant the available resources there, the research expertise of librarians, the information and lists already compiled, and the print and online materials available are sure to save you time and money while you try to figure out how to pay for your own or your child's college education.

ASK AND YE SHALL RECEIVE

What if your library is small, understaffed, or simply doesn't offer much for college research? You can request that resources be added. If the library has a suggestion box or the online equivalent, use it. If not, ask for the name of the head of the reference section, and write that person a letter or e-mail. However you request additional materials, be specific about what you want. You don't need to know the exact resource; you can state your need:

- ✦ "I would like to know more about financial aid programs in our state. Could the library host a class about that?"
- ✦ "I have no idea how to choose a college or help my child to do this. Is there some kind of computer program or website that could help?"
- ✦ "I know that some libraries around the country are offering workshops to help students write the college application essay. Our library should add this type of workshop."

SIX SIMPLE STEPS

For people who haven't used a public library much lately, these should be the first steps you take:

1. If you don't already have a library card, get one. All it takes is a photo ID and proof of address—check with your library to find out exactly what's required. A library card is free, but it acts as the "membership card" that's needed to access materials, including online databases you can search from home, interlibrary loans, and, of course, books, DVDs, and other materials for checkout.

2. Visit your library's website to explore the resources it offers. Browse the entire site to get an overview, and then see if there is a special web page or section devoted to college search, applying to colleges, etc.

3. Go to your library in person to talk to a librarian. Explain that you are looking for help with a financial aid search and ask if there is a college search specialist, a young adult librarian, or a reference librarian who would be the best person to talk to about your search.

4. Some libraries let you schedule an appointment to talk one-on-one with a specific librarian for a set amount of time. If your library does this, by all means make an appointment! If not, find a time when your chosen librarian has some time to talk to you.

5. Ask what resources are available to help you, including compilations of college websites, databases, workshops or classes, college application essay review, etc. Your library may also offer lists of community resources that can help you.

6. Finally, learn how to physically find the resources—books, periodicals, reference materials, etc.—that you'll be using in your search. Explore your library and note where college search information can be found.

THE LAST WORD

Libraries are continually changing and adding to the resources they offer. Even in times of tight budgets and reduced staff, they will find ways to share information, even if it is simply a photocopied list of local resources or websites on a specific topic. So if you think you know what your library has to offer for your college search based on what you found last year—don't be too sure. Head straight back to the reference desk and check out what's new.

Choosing a College

> I chose to go to a community college mostly because I could afford it. It was also close to my house, and I could continue to work. I looked at Alverno College in Milwaukee, but I couldn't deal with the cost and the commute. Because of the articulation agreement in Illinois, my community college credits transferred no problem to a four-year school in the state. I started out at Northern Illinois University as a junior.
> **—Nancy L. McDonald, author and activist**

DON'T OVERLOOK RETENTION AND GRADUATION RATES

While you're checking out the male-to-female ratio at your chosen schools, remember to also check two other figures: retention rate and graduation rate.

The retention rate tells you what percentage of freshman come back after their first year. The graduation rate tells you what percentage of students begin as freshmen and actually graduate at the end of four years.

Both these figures can help you get a better picture of the quality of your school and how satisfied students are with the college's programs.

—from information at CollegeBoard.com

COMPARE: BIG SCHOOLS VS. LITTLE SCHOOLS

College Toolbox: The Advantages and Disadvantages of Both Big and Small Colleges

Think you know everything there is to know about big schools and small schools? Guess again. You may be surprised by the advantages and disadvantages that the College Board found with each one. Obviously, these points don't apply to every school.

Big Schools 101

Advantages

- ✦ There are well-known teachers and famous authors on the faculty.
- ✦ There are many majors and courses to choose from.
- ✦ You can select plenty of different living arrangements, not just dorms.
- ✦ Their big libraries contain hundreds of thousands of volumes.
- ✦ Their big-time sports programs may or may not be on ESPN.
- ✦ There is a huge variety of things to do, both social and academic.

Disadvantages

+ Big-name faculty may not actually teach the classes. Their TAs will.
+ Classes are held in large auditoriums.
+ There are more rules and regs to keep all the students in line.
+ Some faculty are more interested in their research than in undergraduates.
+ It's possible to feel as if you are invisible.
+ Students who did well in high school are now pressured to be A students in college.

Little Schools 101

Advantages

+ Fewer students equals smaller class size.
+ Classes are taught by faculty.
+ Faculty and staff get to know students well.
+ There is a strong bond among students.
+ You may have the chance to design your own major.
+ Small classes mean more discussion and less lecturing.

Disadvantages

+ There are fewer options for academic and social activities.
+ Campuses have smaller buildings and fewer facilities (such as computer labs and libraries).
+ There are not many opportunities to watch or play sports.
+ Dorms are the only housing option.
+ There is a limited number of majors and classes.

WHICH DO YOU PREFER?

Big schools and little schools both have much to offer to students. Your decision is based on which option is the best choice for you considering your career goals, your study style, and your social skills.

COLLEGE LIFE?: ASK A LIBRARIAN

If you want to know exactly what it's like to attend Boston University in Boston or Columbia University in New York City or even DePaul in Chicago, ask your local librarian.

Reference librarians can help you and your parents find books, websites, and blogs that will spell out exactly what it's like to spend your days at BU, Columbia, or DePaul.

Whether you go to school on the West Coast, the East Coast, or somewhere in between, your local librarians can help you find out everything you want to know about living there.

COLLEGES WITH A PARTICULAR SLANT

Maybe you don't care so much about big schools or small schools or East Coast or West Coast. You're looking for a different type of school, a school with a special interest.

If this is true of you, you may want to research the following types of special interest schools:

✦ Single sex

About a hundred schools across the country are still single sex. One of them might be right for you if you don't want the distraction of the opposite sex.

✦ Religious

A variety of colleges are affiliated with a specific religion. You can search the Internet to find colleges for your faith.

✦ Historically black colleges

If you are African American, attending a historically black college may be right for you if you want to be one of the majority instead of the minority. Attending a historically black college could prove to be an eye-opening experience for white students as well.

✦ Hispanic-serving colleges

According to the federal government, a college can be called Hispanic-serving if Hispanic students comprise 25 percent of the undergraduate students.

COLLEGE CONSIDERATIONS

Choosing a college is a huge responsibility. For that reason, it's a good idea to take some time to think about it and to put your thoughts in order.

Although your parents are probably going to help you pay for college, the decision about where to go to school isn't really theirs to make. It's yours. People are correct when they say that the decision can affect the rest of your life.

However, choosing college isn't like choosing a mate. There isn't just one perfect college for you. There are a variety of colleges that can help you turn your dreams into reality. In addition, there are some that can do that as well as meet your other desires such as location, climate, and programs of study.

The difficulty, of course, is knowing your own mind. To choose a college, you need to know enough about yourself to know where you are likely to feel comfortable and where you will feel out of place. That doesn't mean that you have to choose a college environment just like the environment you grew up in.

If you grew up in the suburbs, for example, you may decide that you'd like to try something completely different and think about attending school in Big Sky Country in the West. By the same token, you may decide to stray a little from your normal urban vibe and attend a prestigious college in a small town in the East. You may decide to stay right in your own town and attend the local community college for two years.

All of these are perfectly good options, and in every case you would be getting an excellent education. The difference is in what would make you happy and make you feel the most comfortable.

Use the checklist at the end of this chapter to keep track of which schools have the options that you want. The chart can also help you figure out which options are the most important to you.

Campus Visits: Find Out the Skinny on Your College with This Top Ten List

In a short campus visit, it's difficult to know if the college will be right for you or not. To make sure that you haven't missed anything significant during your tour, follow this top-ten checklist from the College Board.

1. Wander around the campus by yourself.
2. Spend one night in a dorm room.
3. Scan bulletin boards to see what student life might be like.
4. Eat in the cafeteria.
5. Read the student newspaper.
6. Look for other student publications such as literary magazines, alternative newspapers, or departmental newsletters.

7. Ask random students what they love and hate about the school.
8. Listen to the college's radio station.
9. Browse in the college bookstore.
10. Search for your favorite book in the library.

Four-Year or Two-Year?

The first choice you have to consider is if you want to attend a four-year or two-year school. The truth is that if you attend a two-year school, also called a community college, you will ultimately be transferring to a four-year school as a junior.

The good news is that four-year schools are tough when it comes to admitting freshman, but much less tough when admitting junior transfer students. So, you can get your two-year degree at a community college and still end up graduating from your first-choice school.

Four-year Much is written about the joys of attending the same college for the full four years. It's a chance to find yourself, to make friends for a lifetime, and to fashion a career for yourself. It can also be a time when you're homesick, annoyed with your roommate, and wishing that you'd been nicer to your younger siblings. In short, those four years of school in the same location are pretty much what you make of them.

In this case, you need to understand enough about yourself to know if you will find that whole new life a worthwhile challenge or a hurdle too tall to leap. As with everything else, it depends on your attitude.

Two-year For many years, two-year colleges—community colleges—have gotten a bad rap. However, in difficult economic times, most students can understand the idea of a reasonable tuition rate with the option to work and still live at home.

What many students don't realize is that the education at community colleges is first rate. Class sizes are small and usually taught by faculty, not teaching assistants. In addition, many faculty are ready and willing to help if students encounter difficulty with the subject.

Myth Busters: The Top Five Myths About Community Colleges

If you think that your local community college is just high school with ashtrays, check out the truth behind these five common misconceptions.

Myth #1: I won't get financial aid at community college.

Truth: Financial aid is available for students at any accredited college. The tuition at community colleges is low, but students who need financial aid can get it. They fill out the FAFSA just as the students at four-years schools do.

Myth #2: I won't be able to hack a "real" college after attending community college.

Truth: According to recent research, students who transfer from community colleges do as well as or better than students who have attended that college for all four years, although some students can experience a transfer shock of a half a grade point average.

Myth #3: Community college credits don't transfer to four-year schools.

Truth: Actually, they do. Many four-year schools have articulation agreements with community colleges, which makes transferring credits easier.

Myth #4: Community college is only for people majoring in HVAC or other vocational-technical majors.

Truth: Not true. You can study any number of liberal arts and sciences at a community college. Community colleges were set up in the first place to offer college classes at a reasonable price. The idea was that students would spend two years at a community college and then transfer to a four-year school.

Myth #5: Only losers go to community college.

Truth: Lots of famous people have attended community college including the following:

+ Sam Shepard, Pulitzer Prize–winning playwright
+ James Sinegal, CEO of Costco
+ Jim Lehrer, news anchor
+ Maxwell Taylor, former Chairman of the Joint Chiefs of Staff
+ Jeanne Kirkpatrick, former United Nations ambassador
+ Gwendolyn Brooks, Pulitzer Prize–winning author
+ Eileen Collins, NASA astronaut
+ Robert Moses, dance company founder and choreographer

—based on information from the College Board

Public or Private?

Your second big decision is if you want to go to a public or private college. In general, public colleges are called universities and are funded by tax money. Private schools are not funded by tax dollars. In most cases, the public schools are larger, and the private schools are smaller.

However, this doesn't hold true for every school in either camp.

Public Public schools include some of the biggest schools in the country and some of the toughest to get into. The University of Illinois, for example, is a public school, and it is difficult to be admitted. However, a variety of public universities are not particularly difficult to get into, and they offer a wide variety of majors to choose from.

Public colleges and universities offer a huge variety of options if you don't exactly know what you want to major in. They are also quite cost-effective. They offer many options for extracurricular events and college nightlife—depending on their location.

Private In general, private schools are smaller than public ones. However, private schools are usually more selective when choosing which students to admit. Depending on where they are located, private schools can offer the same activities and nightlife as public schools.

Smaller schools can also offer smaller classes and more chance that you will get to know the faculty. You may get to know almost all of your classmates, as well, if the school is small enough.

Size of School

While most students do not choose a school solely because of its size, size does matter. For example, a very large school can offer more extracurricular activities and even some television-worthy sports teams to watch. A bigger school usually has a larger library with more books, more classrooms and lab facilities, and more dormitories.

In the midst of all those students, you may feel anonymous. If you're from a small town, you may like the feeling. If you want everyone to know your name, you may not like it.

With a small school, you may feel that everyone knows your business. The faculty may know you by name, but if you didn't do well on midterms they will all know that as well. You're also less likely to meet a diverse bunch of people at a very small school.

However, you need to choose a size that will make you feel comfortable. When you're comfortable, you feel confident and are ready to learn.

ASK A LIBRARIAN

Librarians are the perfect people to ask about choosing a college. They can help you find information about systematic ways to choose a school or how to know exactly how you feel about the decision.

If you want books or websites or databases, your local library is the place to go to find out everything there is to know about choosing the right college for yourself or your child.

Cost of School

While it would be nice to live in a world where the cost didn't matter, in our world just the opposite is true.

Just as with the size of the school, most students do not choose a college based only on the costs. But costs do matter.

Obviously, if you live near your hometown, transportation to and from school will be cheaper as will the cost of moving in. Living farther away from school probably means fewer trips home.

The trick is to find a school that offers most of the things you want at a price that you and your parents can afford. Don't forget, however, about financial aid. If the costs of school are higher, the financial aid package is also higher.

You don't have to accept all the financial aid you are offered or sign up for the loans you qualify for. You can decide to work while at school or otherwise pay for school yourself.

Type of Environment

One of the bigger decisions about your college is what type of environment you want. Do you want to live in or near a big city? Do you want to be able to hike or participate in outdoor activities? Do you want to see a part of the country that you've only read about?

All of these things are possible when you're looking at schools. You just need to have some idea of what you're looking for.

Urban Every major city in the United States has first-rate colleges and universities nearby or inside the city limits. This is even true of cities overseas. You may decide on an urban college because it's the opposite of where you grew up or because your career epicenter is in big cities. You may also decide on an urban school because that school offers just exactly the major or program that you want.

Urban schools are usually easy to get around in, because there is public transportation. There's nightlife, too, in an urban setting, and a chance to see the latest art show, play, or musical performance.

Suburban Suburban schools offer the proximity to big cities without the congestion and parking headaches. Frequently, students drive to suburban campuses, although there can also be a bus system.

Suburban schools are also perfectly placed to allow you to get to the city to see the latest events, hear important speakers, and meet people who can help you in your career. Suburban schools offer a nice middle ground between the urban and rural environments because you can do either or both, depending on what you need or want.

Rural Rural environments are perfect for those who love outdoor sports or want to major in something related to the outdoors. You can still get to a city, but the wide-open spaces can offer peace and tranquillity that can be hard to find in urban settings.

Smaller towns and fewer people can also be relaxing. Life in rural towns can go a bit more slowly, and few people are racing to get to the next event.

Geography and Climate

Frequently, students choose a college so that they can see another part of the country or enjoy a completely different climate. If the college that offers the coursework you want is located in a perfect climate, it certainly makes for a win-win decision.

Region No matter where you grew up, you may decide to try something different by living in a different part of the country for four years. You may decide to stay in the same geographic region but move over a state or two to attend school.

Whatever you decide, you need to think carefully about what will make you comfortable and what kinds of activities you like.

For example, if you hate every winter sport, it's probably not a good idea to think about colleges in Minnesota or Wisconsin.

Climate If you grew up in the Midwest, you may decide to spend your college years in California to escape snow. You may also decide that because you like hockey, you ought to move someplace where hockey is king.

Whatever your reasoning, make sure that you're choosing a college for a variety of reasons and not just because you can wear a bikini to class.

Being close to home Frequently, students want to move far, far away from home. The thinking is that if you are far away, you will be able to manage things for yourself and really grow up. No matter how close or far you are from home, you are going to grow up. It's inevitable.

The question for you to answer is how often you want to return home to visit family and friends. Going to school across the country makes this more difficult and more costly.

Academics and Prestige

Choosing a college because it offers the program or major that you want makes perfect sense. In fact, it would be nice if this were one of your top five college considerations. If your school of choice also happens to be one of the Ivy League schools (Brown University, Columbia University, Cornell University, Dartmouth College, Harvard University, Princeton University, the University of Pennsylvania, and Yale University) or a member of the select Seven Sisters colleges (Barnard College, Bryn Mawr College, Mount Holyoke College, Radcliffe College, Smith College, Vassar College, and Wellesley College), that's all the better.

Since you are presumably going to college to start a career, not just get a job, it makes sense to choose a college based on how it can help your future career prospects. Ivy League schools and Seven Sister colleges have been shown to help people establish themselves no matter their career.

However, a good education at a school with a specific professor, a particular department, or a special program is also a way to establish yourself in your future career.

It's also a good idea to check the teacher-to-student ratio. Colleges often list this information on their websites.

Miscellaneous Considerations

Along with the obvious considerations concerning college location and distance from home, most students also think about where their friends or loved ones are going to school. Here are some additional things that you may want to consider.

Parents You may want to attend a particular college because your parents went there. You may also think about a particular school because your parents will only pay if you attend that college. There's even a possibility that you want to attend a school because one or both parents couldn't get admitted to it. Whatever the reason, remember that it's your education and your choice.

Friends It may be tempting to go to college with your best friend or friends. However, you will make friends wherever you go to school. That will be easier if you are on your own.

Again, choose a college because it's right for you and your career goals, not because everyone else is going there.

Siblings Going to the same school as your brother or sister makes a certain kind of sense to parents. They only have to drive to one location to pick up both kids. Your sibling can help you move in and vice versa. In fact, your sibling can help you get settled in and walk you around the campus.

However, your sibling won't be around to help you for the rest of your life. Sometimes it's important to do things all on your own to prove to yourself (and others) that you can. Your task is to figure out if attending college is one of those prove-yourself-to-yourself moments.

Boyfriend or girlfriend Although going to the same college as your friends is tempting, going to the same college as your boyfriend or girlfriend can be a tug-of-war. You want to be with the one you love, but you also want to do something just for yourself.

Common wisdom has it that your relationship won't make it through the long distance and time apart. Only you can decide what's the right decision for you to make about your future.

Just answer one question: If you go to the same college as your beloved, what happens if you break up?

Student life/nightlife All colleges, no matter how small, have nightlife and campus activities. Bigger schools tend to have more to do. Don't choose a school just because it has a "party" reputation. You are, after all, supposed to be attending college in order to graduate and start a career.

That said, feel free to ask about nightlife and activities when you visit the college. Ask what people do on the weekends. Ask if it's boring. The students who are taking you on the tour of the college may not be perfectly honest with you, so ask any random students that you meet.

In fact, it's a good idea to plan some alone time on campus, so you can walk around, get a feel for the place, and play Twenty Questions with the students you meet. You may be surprised at what you find out.

Best in Show:
The Best Information About
Colleges and Careers

If you want to search various career paths, then JobStar.org is the place for you. You can find out about hundreds of careers and what day-to-day life is like for many professionals.

http://jobstar.org/tools/career/car-lib.php

If you want a digital tool to help you keep track of your college applications, the College Board has the app for you. It's called My Organizer. You can keep track of the schools you'd like to visit and those you want to apply to. Signing up is free.

https://ecl.collegeboard.com/account/login.jsp?applicationId=0&desti nationpage=https%3A%2F%2Fmyorganizer.collegeboard.com%2Fmy_ organizer%2FMyOrganizer.jsp

CHOOSING A COLLEGE WORKSHEET

	School #1	School #2	School #3
Type of School 1:			
Four-Year School			
Two-Year School			
Type of School 2:			
Public			
Private			
Size of School:			
Tiny school (1,000 students or less)			
Small school (1,500– 5,000 students)			
Mid-sized school (5,000–35,000)			
Big School (more than 35,000 students)			
Cost of School:			
Per credit hour			
Room and Board			
Fees			
Travel to and from school			
Type of Environment:			
Urban			
Suburban			
Rural			

	School #1	School #2	School #3
Proximity to Home:			
1–2 hours from home			
2–4 hours from home			
5+ hours from home			
Overseas			
Geographic Region:			
East Coast			
West Coast			
Midwest			
North			
South			
Climate:			
Little Winter			
No Winter			
Lots of Winter			
Prestige:			
Ivy League			
Listed in Top 10 Colleges List			
Seven Sisters			
Teacher-to- Student Ratio			
Major You Want:			
Special Programs			
Specific Professor			

	School #1	School #2	School #3
Specific Major			
Particular Course of Study			
Other Reasons to Choose School:			
Friend(s) go there			
Boyfriend/Girlfriend goes there			
Sibling goes there			
Excellent nightlife			
Good extracurricular programs			
Close to internship opportunities			

Personal Resources to Pay For College

" The smartest thing we ever did was to pay into the prepaid college plan in Virginia. Sure, it was a pain at the time—because it was such an additional expense on top of private school for our two kids—but if we hadn't done it, we wouldn't be able to afford college now with our drastically changed financial situation.
—Shauna Nouhra, small business owner

MYTH BUSTERS

Myth: My folks will have to sell their house to pay for college.

Truth: Calculations for federal aid do not take into consideration the value of your parents' house. Some colleges do take home equity into account when they try to determine how much your family can

contribute to your college costs. However, family income is the biggest factor in aid determination. Colleges do not expect your parents to sacrifice their home for your college education.

—from College Counseling Sourcebook, 4th edition, 2007, and the College Board (www.collegeboard.com)

Factoid: College Graduates Earn More

According to the U.S. Census Bureau, those who graduate from a four-year college or university earn on average $1 million more in their careers than those who only graduate from high school.

In 2005, the median salaries of women who were college graduates were 70 percent higher than the median for those who had only graduated from high school.

For men, during the same period, the median salary was 63 percent higher.

—from www.collegesavings.org

Factoid: College Costs Up 51 percent

The College Board estimates that the average cost of a college education (tuition and fees) at public four-year colleges and universities has increased approximately 51 percent in the last ten years (numbers adjusted for inflation).

How Much Will College Cost?

Before you begin applying for financial aid, scholarships, grants, or any other kind of help to pay for college, you need to figure out two things:

1. How much will your college education cost?

2. What are your personal resources (money that you and your parents have) to pay for it?

Best in Show: The Best Websites for College Cost Updates

What Every Parent Should Know About Paying for College

Each year, the College Board publishes a Trends in Higher Education report along with several one-page summaries of such things as the costs of community colleges, four-year public schools, and four-year private schools. You can download PDF copies of these reports to keep abreast of the costs of higher education.

www.collegeboard.com/trends

The National Center for Education Statistics has a huge amount of information available under the Fast Facts tab on their website. They also publish a yearly report on the condition of education in the United States.

http://nces.ed.gov/fastfacts/display.asp?id=76

College Costs

COLLEGE TOOLBOX: THE FIVE BASIC COSTS OF COLLEGE

Your total student budget (also called college costs) includes five parts:

#1: Tuition and Fees

Tuition and fees are what most people mean when they talk about the costs of college. These costs are the easiest to estimate as most colleges explain them clearly on their websites. If you plan to take more or fewer credit hours than the "average" at your college, you may want to figure these costs for yourself using the college's per-credit-hour rates and fees.

#2: Room and Board

If you live on campus, the college will usually bill you for room and board. The costs for these will be listed prominently on the school's web page.

Don't forget to check out how the "meal plans" work at your school. Many colleges include three meals a day in their fees, while others ask students to choose how many meals they will be eating on-campus.

You may think that you're saving money by eating fewer meals on campus, but you still have to eat. Unless you're planning on munching microwave mac and cheese every day, you'll spend more money eating out than eating on campus.

If you decide to live off-campus, you will need to figure these costs yourself, including a weekly grocery run. Don't forget that you'll have to buy pots, pans, cooking utensils, and plates to eat on, as well as fresh produce.

#3: Books and Supplies

The costs for books and supplies can vary greatly, depending on your major. If you plan to major in English, you'll probably be buying a number of large, heavy books to carry to class. If you're an art major, on the other hand, you will need to buy a variety of art materials, which can become quite pricey.

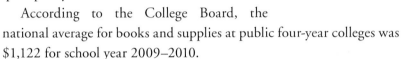

According to the College Board, the national average for books and supplies at public four-year colleges was $1,122 for school year 2009–2010.

#4: Travel

If you live close to college, your travel costs will be minimal. However, many students choose colleges across the country, and their travel costs can add up. In addition, consider the fact that you will want to bring a number of items from home to your dorm room or apartment. Make sure to add in the costs of returning home for school breaks and over the summer to your college costs.

#5: Personal Expenses

Personal expenses such as laundry, cell phone, digital music, take-out food, etc., can really add up, and they are one area where your behavior can make a huge difference to your budget. While you will obviously need to do your laundry every week or so, you can save money by limiting your pizza nights or the number of times per week that you go out with friends.

ASK A LIBRARIAN

Reference librarians can help you and your parents find books, websites, and searchable databases that will spell out exactly what it costs to travel from Yale University back to your sweet home in Chicago or to visit friends in Michigan.

Librarians are also great at finding calculators that can help you determine how much your books and supplies are likely to cost whether you go to school on the West Coast, the East Coast, or somewhere in between.

COLLEGE BUDGETING 101

Budget gurus talk about the two basic types of expenses: fixed and variable. Fixed expenses are the same every month, such as rent, insurance, utilities, etc. Variable expenses can change from month to month such as groceries or entertainment (going out to eat with friends or to a movie).

College expenses also fall into two categories according to the College Board: billable and indirect.

Like fixed expenses, billable costs usually remain the same during the year. For college, these costs include room and board and tuition and fees. In most cases, the college will bill you or your parents for these expenses.

Indirect costs, however, can change a great deal. These are the costs of college that you don't get billed for directly. Indirect costs include expenses such as eating out, monthly cell phone bills, laundry, and travel to and from college. Books and supplies for school (items such as pens, pencils, a computer, notebooks, and art supplies) are also included in indirect costs.

As a student, the costs you have the most control over are the indirect ones. If you restrict your pizza consumption to just once a week, for example, you can save money for an extra trip home or a vacation at spring break. You can also save money on textbooks by buying them online or buying used ones. These small savings can help you in the long run by keeping you from borrowing money and having to pay back loans after college.

PERSONAL RESOURCES

Personal resources include money and other assets that you or your parents can use to pay for your college education. These can include everything from college savings funds to your parents' 401(k) retirement accounts to your own personal savings account, your income from summer jobs, and any savings bonds you've received over the years.

At the end of the chapter, there's a worksheet you can fill out to see exactly how much your college will cost and how much money you and your parents have to pay for those expenses BEFORE you begin applying for financial aid, scholarships, and loans.

Paying for college is often about personal opinions as well as personal resources. Some parents believe that they should pay for all of their children's college education. Other parents believe that the children themselves should be responsible for their college education. One rule of thumb is that parents should expect to pay about a third of their child's college education (some experts suggest half), with financial aid picking up another third, and the last third covered by low-interest student loans.

Factoid: 529 College Savings Plans

College savings plans (often called 529 plans) can be used at colleges and universities across the United States and at some foreign schools. Money from these plans can be used to pay for required college expenses such as books, tuition, fees, supplies, room and board, and equipment.

—www.finaid.org

FOR INSTANCE: IT'S CHEAPER TO SAVE

Clyde and Stella are the proud parents of a beautiful girl. Stella's mother started saving for the baby's college education just as soon as she heard that she was going to be a grandmother.

Her reasoning was clear.

"My great-aunt always said that it was cheaper to save," Stella's mother explains. "If I save $200 a month for 10 years at a rate of just 6.8 percent, the baby will have $34,400 to use for college. If the baby has to borrow that money for college instead, she would have to pay about $396 a month—almost double—for 10 years at 6.8 percent interest. I want to give my grandbaby all the help I can for her education."

—based on information from www.finaid.org

Parents' Resources

Many parents use some of their assets to help their children pay for college. However, before moving forward with any of these options, you need to check with your accountant, a financial planner, and the financial aid office of your child's college to make sure that you understand the full range of tax and financial aid advantages and disadvantages.

Retirement plans and 401(k) plans Taking money from a 401(k) is one way to fund your child's college education.

Normally, you would pay a 10 percent early distribution fee if you take money from the account before you are 59½ years old, and this would be in addition to the normal income tax that you would have to pay on the amount you withdraw.

However, if the withdrawal is for a qualified higher education expense for yourself, your spouse, your child, or your grandchild, you don't have to pay the 10 percent fee. In most cases, qualified expenses include such things as room and board, tuition, books, fees, supplies, and equipment for a student enrolled at least half time in an appropriate degree program.

Similarly, many companies allow you take out a loan from your company's retirement plan to pay for qualified college expenses for your spouse, yourself, or your children. In some cases, those with 403(b) plans for public employees can do the same.

The difficulty with taking money from your 401(k) or company retirement plan is that you will not have that money available to you when you retire. And, while you won't be required to pay the 10 percent penalty if you are paying for college expenses, you will need to check with the college's financial aid office to see if the amount you withdraw for college expenses will be counted as income for you or for your child on next year's financial aid application.

Home equity line of credit Using your home as a means of paying for college for your children can be a good idea, especially if you haven't been able to save. One main advantage is that the market value of your house (your primary residence in IRS-speak) is usually not taken into account by the federal financial aid formulas or the financial aid programs at your child's school.

Be sure to take out a home equity line of credit instead of a home equity loan. To the financial aid people, the proceeds from a loan are considered personal assets. Another advantage is that interest on a line of credit can be taken as a deduction on your taxes.

However, the disadvantages also bear consideration. First, the net value of your home in the marketplace is considered by the financial aid programs at some private colleges. Second, the interest rates on equity lines of credit are higher than for federal loans that the government makes to students but lower than the rates of many private loans for education.

Variable life insurance policies Insurance companies often promote this kind of insurance policy as a good way to save for college. These policies mix life insurance with investment accounts that offer tax-deferred advantages.

The main advantage of this type of insurance is that financial aid programs, including federal financial aid, don't consider them as assets. In addition, the policies generally don't have limits on the amount you are allowed to invest, and the parent controls the money at all times. Also, the owner of the policy can borrow from or withdraw contributions without tax or a penalty.

The disadvantage is that these policies are often pricey. The commissions and expenses also tend to be expensive. Some parents find that the fees make this kind of vehicle more expensive than other options to save for college. In general, the premiums are also not deductible, and any withdrawals cause the ultimate value of the policy (the death benefit) to decrease. Finally, many of these plans will not allow you to take money out until after the policy has been in place for twelve or more years.

MYTH BUSTERS

Myth: Financial Aid Penalizes Parents Who Save for College

Truth: While it is true that financial aid programs do count the assets of the parents when considering financial aid for the children, these programs only count a percentage of the parents' assets. In most cases, the top bracket of assessment is only 5.64 percent.

In addition, the formula used to determine financial aid for students ignores the parents' small businesses, retirement plans, and what the family's home is worth in the marketplace.

Savings

Most experts agree that the best way to pay for your children's education is to save for it. However, you do not always have to begin saving the minute the child is born. Included here are a variety of options to help you save no matter what your child's age.

MYTH BUSTERS

Myth: 529 Plans Only Offer Prepaid Tuition

Truth: 529 plans come in two flavors: savings and prepaid tuition. Prepaid tuition offers families the option of paying for tuition in the future at today's prices. Savings plans offer the opportunity to save for college by allowing the money to grow tax-free in the account until the beneficiary is old enough to use the money for college.

When the funds are used for qualified educational expenses such as books, supplies, tuition, fees, or room and board, they are exempt from federal taxes and may be exempt from state taxes, as well.

So far, every state offers one or the other type of 529 plan. Sixteen states offer both types of plans, and Washington State offers only a prepaid tuition plan.

To find out what your state offers, go to www.collegesavings.org/index.aspx.

(For Coverdell Educational Savings Accounts [ESAs], see the section on Trusts in this chapter.)

529 Savings plans Named for a section of the IRS code that created them, 529 savings plans (or 529 plans as they are usually called) were created specifically to help parents, grandparents, and other family members save for college. (See the Myth Busters box to learn about the two types of plans.)

Basically, 529 plans are investment plans that allow families to save for their children's college educations without having to pay state or federal income tax. The funds that are contributed grow tax-free, and withdrawals used for qualified education expenses are also exempt from federal income tax. In most cases, qualified education expenses include room and board, tuition and fees, books, supplies, and equipment required for classes.

It's difficult to talk about these plans in general because they are run by each individual state, and each state can offer different options and tax advantages. For example, all 529 plans offer tax-exempt withdrawals for appropriate educational expenses. In some states, these educational withdrawals are also exempt from state income tax. In fact, some states offer exemption from state financial aid calculators, matching grants, and specific scholarship opportunities for parents who invest in 529 plans in their state of residence.

What can be said for 529 plans as a whole is that they offer many advantages over other savings vehicles. Besides the excellent tax advantage of these plans, the person who opens the plan (the account holder) is always in control of the money—not the beneficiary of the plan.

The beneficiary of the plan can easily be changed within the family. This makes it much easier to pay for the college education of all your children by switching the beneficiaries as each child graduates from college. In addition, these plans are usually protected from bankruptcy proceedings.

A huge advantage for parents who are behind in their college savings is that 529 plans allow parents to make a lump sum contribution for each beneficiary without gift tax complications. See your individual state plan to check the limits to these contributions and any exclusions.

In addition, most states have different plans to choose from based on the age of the beneficiary and various other investment considerations, including tolerance for risk.

The Basics: 529 Plans in a Nutshell

+ You can establish a 529 account for anyone no matter the relationship. You can even create an account to pay for your own college expenses. The beneficiary just has to be a resident alien or U.S. citizen with a valid Social Security or federal tax identification number.

+ More than one account can be set up for each beneficiary. This way friends and family can donate to the college fund. Friends and family can also contribute to any plan.

+ Money from a 529 plan can be used for any eligible educational institution in the country (and some institutions overseas) as long as it is used for qualified education expenses. Colleges or universities need to be eligible to work with the student aid programs for the U.S. Department of Education, which usually means that they are accredited educational facilities.

+ For most states, you can buy 529 plans directly from the state. Some states also allow financial advisers to sell plans.

+ In most cases, either the beneficiary or the account owner has to live in the state where the 529 plan is purchased, but check your state's rules to make certain.

To buy a 529 plan or find out more about what each state offers, go to the website for the College Savings Plans Network at www.collegesavings.org/index.aspx.

Saving in the parents' names In some cases, parents may choose to start a taxable savings account in their own names to pay for their child's college expenses. The advantages to this are that the financial aid implications are lessened in an asset that belongs to the parents, and the parents can maintain complete control of the account. In addition, parents can decide to use the money in the account for something other than educational expenses if they like.

The downside to owning this type of account is that your earnings will incur state and federal taxes and be subject to the capital gains laws.

Savings social networking programs, credit card rebates, and loyalty programs A variety of companies offer incentive plans that allow friends, family, and even casual acquaintances of students to help them save for college. Some of these programs are so new that the results are not yet in on their effectiveness. However, the tried-and-true nature of rebate and loyalty programs makes it possible for friends and family to do their regular shopping and still help with college expenses. Although none of these programs will pay for an entire college education, many of them can help.

With the advent of social networking sites such as Twitter, Facebook, MySpace, LinkedIn, and others, savings social networking plans are making their debut in the marketplace. Think of them as a bridal registry for college students.

Students sign up and include a list of people they hope will contribute to their fund. The website sends messages to all these potential "sponsors" and asks them to contribute to the students' account. Most of these sites are free to students but charge a fee for sponsors. In return, students can post their most recent grades, a portfolio of their work, and other materials to show sponsors how they are doing.

So far, only a few sites have managed to stay in business during the economic downturn, including College Piggy (www.collegepiggy .com), Freshman Fund (www.freshmanfund.com), and Grade Fund (www.gradefund.com). To protect students from online predators, the student information can be restricted to only those people the student already knows.

Loyalty or affinity programs have been around for a long time, but they have only recently been used to help fund a college education. The idea is that you register your credit and debit cards with a company. When you use your cards to buy certain products or buy from certain stores, a rebate will be sent to the college fund of your choice. The program tracks your spending, and you can often share any rebates among several college funds.

The biggest programs include the following:
+ BabyCenter (www.babycenter.com)
+ BabyMint (www.babymint.com)
+ FutureTrust (www.futuretrust.com)
+ MyKidsCollege (www.mykidscollege.com)
+ SAGE Tuition Rewards Program (www.sagescholars.com)
+ Fidelity 529 College Rewards MasterCard (www.fidelity.com/ college)

Upromise (www.upromise.com) has the one of the biggest networks of retailers, and Upromise was recently purchased by student loan giant Sallie Mae. As of 2007, you can earmark your rebates to pay off the student loan balances of those you love.

Educational Tax Credits

A variety of educational tax credits can also help parents pay for college. Although the parents will have to pay for college expenses first, there are three programs now that will reimburse some of the costs at tax time.

Here's an overview of each tax credit:

American opportunity credit According to the IRS, you can claim up to $2,500 per student per year for qualified education expenses incurred during that school year. However, you can only claim this credit for the first four years of each student's time in college.

The amount you are allowed to take for this credit depends on your annual income. In most cases, you can take this credit if you are married and filing jointly and your modified adjusted gross income (MAGI) is $180,000 or below. For single people and those who qualify as head of household the MAGI is $90,000.

The student or students you are claiming must be pursuing an undergraduate degree or other recognized education credential and be enrolled at least half time. Also, the student cannot have any felony drug convictions on his or her record.

Qualified education expenses are limited to tuition and fees for this credit.

Hope scholarship credit For this credit, you can claim up to $1,800 per student per year for qualified education expenses incurred during that school year, or $3,600 if your student is enrolled in a college in a Midwestern disaster area. However, you can only claim this credit for the first two years of each student's time in college.

The amount you are allowed to take for this credit depends on your annual income. In most cases, you can take this credit if you are married and filing jointly and your modified adjusted gross income (MAGI) is $120,000 or below. For single people and those who qualify as head of household the MAGI is $60,000.

The student or students you are claiming must be pursuing an undergraduate degree or other recognized education credential and be enrolled at least half time. Also, the student cannot have any felony drug convictions on his or her record.

For this credit, qualified education expenses include tuition and fees required for enrollment and any course-related books, supplies, or equipment.

Lifetime learning credit You can claim up to $2,000 per year for qualified education expenses or $4,000 if your student is enrolled in a college in a Midwestern disaster area. You can also claim this credit for all the years of each student's time in college or for your own classes to improve (or acquire) job skills.

The amount you are allowed to take for this credit depends on your annual income. In most cases, you can take this credit if you are married and filing jointly and your modified adjusted gross income (MAGI) is $120,000 or below. For single people and those who qualify as head of household the MAGI is $60,000.

The student or students you are claiming do not need to be pursuing an undergraduate degree. For this credit, qualified education expenses include tuition and fees required for enrollment and any course-related books, supplies, or equipment.

For more information about how to use these tax credits, go to the Internal Revenue Department's website at www.irs.gov or download a PDF version of their Publication 970, "Tax Benefits for Education."

ASK A LIBRARIAN

If you need to understand how to mix and match your education tax credits with your 529 plans, ask a librarian. He or she can point you in the right direction for websites, books, and brochures that will explain everything you ever wanted to know about the IRS and tax law.

Trusts

Although many people think of trusts and trust funds as instruments of the rich, many middle-class families can benefit from the tax advantages inherent in these vehicles, especially when saving and paying for college. However, talk with your accountant, your lawyer, and a financial planner to make sure you understand the tax and financial aid ramifications of each vehicle.

Coverdell educational savings accounts (ESAs) Originally created as Education IRAs in 1997, Coverdell accounts are actually trusts set up to pay for the education costs of the beneficiary. They are exempt from federal taxes and allow a contribution of $2,000 per year for each beneficiary.

The advantage to this type of account is that the account can be owned either by the parent or the child. In this type of account, companies can contribute to individual accounts as well. In addition, parents can contribute to both a 529 plan and a Coverdell account in the same tax year. And, this type of trust can be coordinated with Education Tax Credits. However, the rule is that you cannot pay the same expenses with two different funds.

Perhaps the biggest advantage of the Coverdell Trust is that you can use it to pay for qualified elementary, secondary, and postsecondary school expenses. Qualified educational expenses include computers, uniforms, supplies, books, transportation, tuition, fees, board, tutoring, and required equipment related to classes.

Crummey trust As in most trusts, money, securities, or property are put into an account "in trust" for another person, usually a minor. An attorney draws up the trust documents, and the donor will choose a trustee to oversee the account. Most trusts end when the beneficiary reaches a certain age (usually 18 or 21) and then the beneficiary can control the money in the entire trust.

In a Crummey Trust, there is no rule that the beneficiary can control the entire trust at age 18 or 21. This gives more control to the donor and the trustee. In fact, this kind of trust can be set up for beneficiaries who are 21 or older. In addition, in this vehicle, the beneficiary can only take out the equivalent of the annual contribution. He or she cannot take over running the trust.

The disadvantage of this kind of trust is that the costs to set up this plan and administer it are quite expensive. In addition, a Crummey Trust is considered to be the property of the beneficiary and will count heavily against the student for financial aid.

2503(c) minor's trust This kind of trust is put into place to hold gifts, money, real estate, or other property in trust for a minor until that child reaches age 21. This kind of vehicle can also be used to pay for college expenses. However, as with the Crummey Trust, the setup and administrative costs are high. Also, the trust is treated as the property of the child and will greatly affect financial aid formulas.

UGMA and UTMA custodial accounts The Uniform Gift to Minors Act (UGMA) created a method for minor children to own securities in a trust format. The advantage is that this type of trust does not require an attorney to draw up the documents or the court to appoint a trustee. State statute established the trust.

The Uniform Transfer to Minors Act (UTMA) is like the UGMA except that the former allows minor children to own property other than securities including such things as patents, fine art, real estate, and royalties.

For both types of trusts, a donor must establish a custodial account by appointing a trustee (also called a custodian) and giving the property to the trust. Then the custodian manages the trust for the child until the child reaches adulthood at either age 18 or 21.

The disadvantages of this type of account are that the student does not have to use the money for college expenses. In addition, any money is considered the asset of the student and will negatively impact financial aid formulas.

The advantage is that the assets in the trust are taxed at the child's rate until the child becomes of age.

Other Financial Vehicles

Here are several other methods that families can use to help children pay for college. Savings bonds and the College Savings Bank CDs are especially grandparent-friendly.

College savings bank (CD) This FDIC-insured certificate of deposit (CD), offered by the College Savings Bank, is guaranteed to give a fixed percentage rate at maturity. The CD is indexed to college costs based on the Independent College 500 Index (IC 500) from the College Board. So, the bank promises that the interest rate on this CD will always be at least 2 percent.

To buy one of these CDs, you need to begin with a minimum of $1,000. After that, you can buy more at $250 increments. If you can afford to begin with $10,000 or more, you can earn .5 percent more interest on the CD.

The biggest advantage to this instrument is that, once it has matured, the student or parents can use it at any college or university. Go to the College Savings Bank website (www.collegesavings.com) for more information.

Savings bonds U.S. savings bonds have been the go-to graduation gift for many years, but the Series EE and Series I bonds can be used to pay for college. The Education Bond Program makes these bonds tax-free when they are used to pay for college expenses or rolled over into a 529 savings plan.

The advantage to these bonds is that they are registered in the parents' names, and parents can buy $30,000 of each type of bond each year. The disadvantage is that qualified education expenses are narrowly defined for these bonds and include only tuition and required fees. Books and room and board are specifically excluded. In addition, the tuition must be for classes required as part of a certificate or degree program.

Parents must also keep meticulous records of the expenses that the bonds paid for, including recording the educational institution, the date the expense was paid, and the amount of the qualified educational expense as well as the bond serial number, the face value, the date issued, the date redeemed, and the total amount of the bond at maturity. For more information, go to the website for Savings Bonds Direct at www. savingsbondsdirect.gov.

Best in Show:
The Best College Cost Calculators

Finaid.org has some of the best calculators out there for figuring out the financing associated with college. Here's their calculator for figuring out the costs of college in the future:

www.finaid.org/calculators/costprojector .phtml

The College Board has a wide variety of calculators to help you figure out financial aid numbers, and their college cost calculator is also helpful.

http://apps.collegeboard.com/fincalc/college_cost.jsp

The College Savings Plan Network is your go-to source for information about saving for college and 529 plans, but it is also a good place to scout the costs of college with their excellent calculator.

www.collegesavings.org/collegeCostCalculator.aspx

COLLEGE COSTS WORKSHEET

	School #1	School #2	School #3
Cost per credit hour			
Fees per credit hour			
Tuition: full-time hours			
Tuition: half-time hours			
Books and School Supplies (full year)			
Room and Board: one semester			
Room and Board: full year			
Room and Board: summer semester			
Travel			
Personal Expenses			

COLLEGE RESOURCES TO PAY FOR COLLEGE WORKSHEET

	Student #1	Student #2	Student #3
Parents:			
401(k) plans			
Retirement plans			
Home equity line of credit			
Variable life insurance policies			
529 savings plans			

	Student #1	Student #2	Student #3
529 prepaid tuition plans			
Savings plans in parents' names			
Affinity or loyalty programs			
Tax Credit: American Opportunity			
Tax Credit: Hope Scholarship			
Tax Credit: Lifetime Learning			
Coverdell ESA (trust)			
Crummey Trust			
College Savings Bank CD			
Savings Bonds			
Students:			
Savings social networking plans			
Affinity or loyalty programs			
Student savings acct			
Coverdell ESA			

	Student #1	Student #2	Student #3
2503(c) Minor's Trust			
UGMA and UTMA Custodial Accounts			
College Savings Bank CD			
Savings Bonds			
Graduation gifts from family and friends			

Financial Aid 101

" One of the more frustrating conversations a financial aid director has with a family is to tell them they applied too late for scarce scholarships and grants. As a result, the only 'package' the aid office can offer is a combination of loans and student employment.

I wish all parents and students would check and double-check the financial aid application deadlines. It is a simple review of the school's website to learn the 'priority application date.' Financial aid offices will make a commitment to provide a full financial aid award to families meeting the priority application date.

—Earl Dowling, financial aid director, Harper College

MYTH BUSTERS

Myth: My school offered me financial aid, so I don't need to apply for federal student aid.

Truth: Many colleges use the FAFSA to determine the financial need for their students. For this reason, all college students need to submit the FAFSA just to see if they qualify for federal, state aid, and aid from their individual schools.

In addition, scholarships and grant programs also rely on the FAFSA information to determine needs-based aid for their applicants.

It can't hurt to submit the FAFSA even if you end up not qualifying for any federal aid.

—from finaid.org

SCAM ALERT: DON'T PAY FOR FREE ASSISTANCE

No organization or company can help you to get more financial aid just by paying a fee or having someone else "submit" your financial aid application.

For help filling out your financial aid forms, go to the financial aid office of your college or ask your high school counselor.

Remember, if you submit incorrect information you will have to pay back your financial aid and may be asked to pay additional fines or fees. Sending false information can result in prison time.

Factoid: Eligibility for Federal Student Aid

To be eligible to receive student aid from the federal government you must NOT:

✦ Have a drug conviction for an offense that happened while you were getting federal student aid such as grants, loans, or work-study monies

✦ Be in default on a federal student loan

✦ Owe a refund for a federal grant

In addition, you MUST:

✦ Be an eligible noncitizen

✦ Be a U.S. citizen

✦ Demonstrate financial need

✦ Have a valid Social Security number

✦ Be registered for the Selective Service (if you are a male 18–25 years old)

✦ Have a high school diploma or a GED certificate

✦ Be enrolled or accepted at a school that participates in the federal student aid program

See your school's financial aid office for other requirements. For more information, you can also download a booklet called *Funding Education Beyond High School: The Guide to Federal Student Aid* at www.studentaid.gov/students/publication/student_guide/index.html.

—from www.fafsa.ed.gov/faq003.htm

Factoid: Hierarchy of Financial Aid

Not all financial aid is created equal. Some aid, such as grants and scholarships, does not have to be paid back. Other aid, such as student loans, has to be paid back after you graduate from college.

Begin your search for financial aid by figuring out what you can contribute and then what your parents can contribute. After you've figured that out, look for scholarships and grants to pay for as much as you can.

Once you've exhausted all those options, consider work study at your college, a paid internship, or getting a job while you are in school or during the summers.

After you have looked at every other option, consider taking out a student loan for any additional expenses. Although college graduation seems far away now, remember that you'll have to pay back any loans soon after you graduate.

In general, the rates are lower for students who take out student loans than for parents who take out loans to pay for their children's education.

WHERE DO I START WITH FINANCIAL AID?

Once you've completed the worksheets in chapter 2, you should have a good idea of how much your college education will cost and how much you and your parents can contribute toward those costs.

In this chapter, we'll consider how to apply for financial aid. For most students, applying for financial aid means filling out the Free Application for Federal Student Aid (FAFSA). Because this resource is available from the government, many schools use it to figure out the financial aid that they will give their students. In fact, a number of scholarships and grants also use the FAFSA (pronounced faaf-SUH) to figure out which students have the most financial need.

For this reason, financial aid experts advise all college-bound students to fill out the FAFSA online. Even if you don't get federal financial aid, you may be eligible for state financial aid or specific aid from your school. Financial aid also includes the opportunity to participate in work-study programs at your school.

CAVEAT: If you want to fill out the FAFSA on paper, you can do so. Print out the document from this website (www.fafsa.ed.gov). Sign it. Mail it to the address listed on the website.

However, the instructions in this chapter refer to filling out the online FAFSA form. Filling out the FAFSA online saves you about fourteen days, especially if you sign the online form with a PIN.

DEADLINE ALERT: FINANCIAL AID DEADLINES

You and your parents can submit the FAFSA starting on **January 1** every year. Financial aid advisers suggest that you and your parents get your taxes done BEFORE January 1 so that you can fill out the FAFSA online in the early days of January.

Although your school and your state may have other deadlines, many of them will not make their financial aid decisions until they see the results of the FAFSA.

So, if you think you'll need financial aid to go to college, you want to be the early bird.

Financial Aid Tips: Five Tips to Get Your Money Quickly

1. Apply Early.

Every state and every school is different. However, you can't go wrong by starting early and knowing the due dates for your state and your specific school.

Financial aid runs out in most schools, so applying early will help you get a piece of the financial aid pie.

2. Find out if you need other forms.

Check with your college's financial aid office to see if you need to fill out additional forms. While many schools use the FAFSA results to determine who gets aid, other schools use their own individual forms. Also, check your individual state to see if state-specific forms are required to get financial aid.

3. Read the fine print.

This means reading and rereading the instructions. Make sure you understand what the FAFSA means by specific financial aid terms such as "household" and "dependent student" before you fill out the forms.

4. Complete your tax return early.

If the FAFSA people have questions, they will ask you or your parents to verify your answers to the FAFSA questions. In most cases, what you will need is your tax returns. You and your parents can save yourselves a great deal of stress by getting your taxes done early.

For most questions, you will be directly transferring data from your tax return to the FAFSA online form. If you don't get your taxes done early, you will need to enter incomplete data into the FAFSA, and you will have to correct this information once you do file your tax returns.

Doing your taxes in advance means that you will not have to wait for your FAFSA results until you have submitted the correct tax information.

5. File electronically.

Filling out your FAFSA online saves you at least fourteen business days over mailing in a paper form. According to the FAFSA website, the FAFSA online form edits your application and this ensures that the data you submitted is ready to be processed.

Factoid: Tax Info and Financial Aid

You will need tax information for yourself and your parents for the year BEFORE you want to attend school.

So, for example, if you were planning to attend college in the 2010–2011 academic year, you would need to provide tax information for 2009. And, if you wanted to begin college during school year 2012–2013, you would need to show your own and your parents' income by providing information from the 2011 tax forms.

—www.fafsa.ed.gov

Factoid: How Do Schools Get My FAFSA Information?

In the online FAFSA form, students can list up to ten schools that they want their FAFSA information sent to. There's an online listing, so you can search for the name of each school.

FAFSA ONLINE: SUPPORTED BROWSERS

The following operating systems and browsers are certified for use with FAFSA on the web.

Using other operating systems or browsers may cause the pages to display improperly on your computer or you may have problems entering data into the application.

+ Apple Safari Browsers: Apple Safari 3.1 and Apple Safari 4.0
+ America Online Browsers: AOL 8.0, 9.0, AOL Explorer 2.0, and AOL Explorer 1.5
+ Mozilla Firefox Browsers: Firefox 1.5, Firefox 2.0, and Firefox 3.5
+ Microsoft Browsers: Internet Explorer 6.0, Internet Explorer 7.0, and Internet Explorer 8.0.

See this URL for more specific information about operating systems: *www.fafsa.ed.gov/FOTWwebApp/beforebrowser_req.jsp.*

Step One: Gather Documents

As with most other things in life, you can save yourself time and aggravation by preparing in advance to fill out the FAFSA. Here's what you'll need:

+ Your driver's license number
+ Your Social Security number
+ Your W-2 forms and any other record of income for the PRIOR year
+ If you are married, you will need you and your spouse's Federal Income Tax Return for the PRIOR year.

+ If you are a dependent student, you will need your parents' Federal Income Tax Return for the PRIOR year.

+ Records for any untaxed income from the PRIOR year

+ Your current bank statements

+ Investment mortgage information, self-employed business forms, bonds or other investment records for you, your spouse if you are married, and your parents if you are a dependent student.

+ If you are not a U.S. citizen, you need to provide your alien registration or permanent resident card.

You can start and stop while you're filling out the FAFSA online, and the website will save your progress. However, you can easily fill out the form in one sitting if you have the correct documents prepared in advance.

MYTH BUSTERS

Myth: It's going to take me weeks to find the information and fill out the FAFSA form, even online. There must be an easier way.

Truth: Nope. Gathering the information, filling out the web worksheet ahead of time, and then going online to fill out the FAFSA on the web is the fastest method to complete the form.

On average, the experts at Federal Student Aid estimate that it will take about an hour and fifteen minutes to complete the online FAFSA form. Filling out the form online also makes it faster for you to get your results and to make any corrections to the information.

—from www.fafsa.ed.gov

Step Two: Apply for a PIN

While it is still possible to fill out the FAFSA on paper, sign the forms with a pen, and mail it to its destination, it is much easier and much faster to fill out the forms online and sign them with a digital signature, called a PIN. If you are a dependent student, your parents will need to apply for one, as well, because they also need to sign your FAFSA.

A PIN is a four-digit number that is assigned to you. This number allows you to:

+ Sign your FAFSA,
+ See the results of the FAFSA on the website,
+ Apply for financial aid in future years, and
+ Access other federal financial aid websites.

Although you can apply for a PIN while you are filling out the FAFSA online, it's more convenient to apply for one while you are in the process of gathering documents and information for the online form. That's because the information you submit to get your PIN has to be verified by the Social Security Administration. If you apply for a PIN while you're online, the PIN is conditional, and all you can do with it is sign your FAFSA.

Go to www.pin.ed.gov to apply for a PIN. It takes one to three days for the number to be verified, but you can use that time to gather your documentation and begin filling out the web worksheet.

Security Information: Keeping Your PIN Secure

Your PIN is important. Besides signing your FAFSA with it, you can use it to make binding legal obligations and access your personal records.

Also, you only need to apply for it once during your entire college career. You and your parents (if you are a dependent student) can use the same PIN to sign the FAFSA every year and view the results.

So, keep your PIN safe and be sure you know where to find it for next year's FAFSA.

> *NOTE:* If you apply for your PIN while you're online filling out the FAFSA, you can view your PIN instantly or have it e-mailed to you. However, that PIN is considered to be conditional. The Social Security Administration has to verify your information and that can take from one to three business days. All you can do with the instant-read PIN is sign your FAFSA.

After the PIN is verified, you can use it to look at your FAFSA information or access additional federal student aid websites.

Step Three: Complete the Web Worksheet

Okay, here's where all this preparation is going to seem a little silly. You've gathered all these documents so that you can go online and fill out the FAFSA, right?

Uh, not so much. All the documents are so that you can fill out a web WORKSHEET.

Trust me, filling out the worksheet FIRST makes it a breeze to fill in the information online. In fact, you can pretty much just transfer the data from the worksheet to the online form.

So, first, print out the four-page web Worksheet at www.fafsa. ed.gov/before001.htm.

Here's a preview of what you'll see:

Section 1: student information This section asks for student information including citizenship status, Social Security number, marital status, drug convictions, and Selective Service registration (for men).

Section 2: student dependency information If a student can check any of these boxes, he or she is not a dependent student and can skip straight to section 4.

Section 3: parent information This section starts with a long definition of who qualifies as a parent. Parents will need to provide their Social Security numbers, their names, and their dates of birth. In addition, this section asks for tax information.

Section 4: student tax information Here students report their adjusted gross income and other tax information.

ASK A LIBRARIAN

Financial aid forms are complicated—even the online version of the FAFSA. If you need help, go to your local library, and ask the closest librarian to suggest some books, e-books, websites, brochures, or databases that will help you fill out the forms.

Better yet, ask your local library to host a seminar or workshop to help local parents understand the forms and fill them out. Ask them to invite professionals from the closest college financial aid office to come and speak.

The library is there to help, so ask.

Step Four: Fill Out the FAFSA Online

Now that you have all the documents in hand AND you've filled out the web Worksheet, you can go to the website (www.fafsa.gov) to fill out the online form.

The online form will allow you to use various calculators if you need them, and there is also an online help feature every step of the way. The NEED HELP? button is available on every screen, and tips will appear on the right-hand side of the form as you are filling it in. There's also a live help feature at the bottom of each page.

You can also stop and save your FAFSA, and the website will save your progress for forty-five days.

Also, the FAFSA form online tells you exactly what line on your tax returns you need to use to fill in each blank of the financial data.

Before submitting the online form, check every box to make sure that you've filled it out correctly. If the information isn't correct, you will need to make corrections to it later, and that can delay your financial aid.

INACCURATE INFORMATION: YOU PLAY AND YOU PAY

You need to submit correct information on the FAFSA and all other financial aid documents so that you can get all the financial aid you are entitled to. In most cases, you will be asked to verify the information you provide online with federal tax documents.

Unfortunately, if you provide incorrect information, you could be asked to pay back any financial aid that you get along with fines and fees. According to the FAFSA website, if you purposely give false or misleading information on your application, you could be fined $20,000, sent to prison, or both.

FAFSA INFO: SAVE YOUR CONFIRMATION PAGE

When you submit your FAFSA online, you will be shown a confirmation page with a confirmation number on it.

Print this page out and save it for your records. The confirmation number proves that you filled out the FAFSA online and includes the date and time that you sent the form to the Department of Education.

You can also have a copy of this form e-mailed to you for your records.

Step Five: Sign the Form Electronically with a PIN

You can sign your FAFSA three different ways, but using a PIN is the fastest way to get your results.

However, you can also print out the signature page, sign it (along with your parents if you are a dependent student), and mail it in after submitting your FAFSA online.

A final method is to wait until you receive your Student Aid Report (SAR) from the Department of Education and then sign and return it via mail.

Step Six: Get Your Results

Once you get your confirmation page, you know that your form has been submitted, and you just need to wait for the results.

However, for those of you who don't want to wait until you see the official results, you can check the status of your application online.

+ If you signed the FAFSA with a PIN, you can check the status of your application just one week after submitting it.
+ If you printed, signed, and mailed a hard copy of the signature form, you can check the status of your form two to three weeks after submitting the form.

In about a month, you will get a paper copy of your Student Aid Report (SAR) or you will be e-mailed one if you have included your e-mail address.

The SAR lists an Expected Family Contribution (EFC), which is a preliminary estimate based on the information in your FAFSA. This indicates what your family can be expected to contribute to your school expenses.

Your SAR (with the EFC) will be sent to all the schools you indicated on the FAFSA. You can include more schools and get extra copies of your SAR online.

You need your PIN (electronic signature) number in order to be able to view your SAR and to have it sent to additional schools.

Best in Show: Financial Aid Websites

www.students.gov

This is the student gateway to the U.S. government. You can find information about the financial aid options for each state and other pertinent information about the government that affects students.

www.studentaid.ed.gov

Find out everything you ever wanted to know about federal student aid to students and how it works on this government website.

www.fastweb.com

This website has a hip style, but it also explains how to get financial aid and what types of aid are available for college students today.

www.finaid.org

If you want an explanation of any part of the financial aid process, this is the website for you. Everything is explained clearly and concisely.

Step Seven: Make Corrections

Once you get the results from the FAFSA, you can make corrections.

You may want to correct information that was not accurate on the original form. In addition, you may want to make changes if your family situation changes (for example, your parents divorce).

If you have a PIN, you can make changes electronically to your FAFSA information.

Step Eight: Await Your Financial Aid Package

Once your FAFSA has been processed and you've received your SAR, the financial aid office at your college will begin putting together a financial aid package for you. This may include financial aid from the school, the state, the federal government, scholarships, grants, work-study programs, and school loans.

You do not have to accept everything that the financial aid office offers to you. For example, you and your parents may decide not to take out a student loan at the beginning of your college career or at all.

FAFSA Info: A Word About Special Circumstances

If the financial circumstances for you or your family have changed since you filled out the online FAFSA, you can make changes electronically to your information if you have already applied for and received a PIN.

In addition, if you or your parents disagree with the SAR or EFC, you can explain your special circumstances to the FAFSA team. Special circumstances can include the fact that you or your parents have divorced since you filled out the FAFSA, one or both parents have lost their jobs, or you or your parents have incurred unusual dental or medical expenses during the year.

According to the Department of Education, the following situations are not considered special circumstances:

✦ You do not live with your parents.

✦ Your parents refuse to contribute to your college expenses.

✦ Your parents do not want to provide their tax information on the FAFSA.

✦ Your parents do not claim you as a dependent on their taxes.

For more information about what constitutes special circumstances, go to the FAFSA website at www.fafsa.ed.gov.

A GLOSSARY OF FINANCIAL AID TERMS

✦ Data Release Number (DRN)

The Department of Education assigns a number to your application. If you file the FAFSA online, this number will be included on your confirmation page. You need the DRN to change your mailing address or to add more schools you want to receive your SAR.

✦ Expected Family Contribution (EFC)

This is the amount that the Department of Education believes that your family can contribute to your college costs. It's listed in the SAR. Your ability to get financial aid is based on the Cost of Attendance (what it will cost for you to attend college) and then your family's EFC is subtracted from that.

✦ FAFSA

Free Application for Federal Student Aid. This is an online form that all college students need to fill out. Many schools use it to figure out state aid, school aid, and scholarship aid to students.

✦ FAFSA transaction

When you submit your FAFSA or make a correction to it, a transaction number is created. Each time a new transaction is noted by the FAFSA system, they send you an SAR. In addition, the Department of Education sends an SAR to the schools you indicated in your form.

✦ Federal Methodology

This is the formula that FAFSA uses to figure out your family's EFC on your SAR. It is based on the Higher Education Act of 1965.

✦ Financial Need

This is what the financial aid office at your school will figure out based on your SAR and the cost of attending that school.

✦ Needs Assessment

This is the FAFSA and any other financial aid form that indicates how much money you will need to attend college. Many states and colleges have their own needs assessment forms.

✦ PIN

This is a four-digit number that you can use to sign your FAFSA electronically and to view your SAR or correct information on your FAFSA.

✦ Signature Page

This page is required by the Department of Education. You can use an electronic signature (a PIN) to sign it or print out and sign a paper form. The paper form has to be mailed to the Department of Education.

✦ Student Aid Report (SAR)

The SAR is the report that tells you, your parents, and your college how much your parents can give you to go to college (the EFC). Based on the information in this report, the financial aid office at your college will create a financial aid package for you.

✦ Work study

This is a financial aid program at your individual school that allows students to work on campus during the school year and be paid from financial aid money provided by the college.

Scholarships

I fell into getting a scholarship for college because my English teacher told me about this essay contest. I wrote the essay only because I wanted to get published. Not only did my essay get published, but the sponsors of the contest, The Soroptimist Club, gave me $500 for college—every year. And they even sponsored a dinner in my honor, so I could meet the rest of the members. They introduced me as if I was Secretary General of the U.N., and I've never forgotten them or their unlooked-for help. That $500 bought my books every year.

**—Heather Z. Hutchins, freelance writer and
blogger at www.examiner.com**

MYTH BUSTERS

Myth: Scholarships only go to athletes, musicians, or class valedictorians. I don't have a chance against people like that.

Truth: Scholarships come in all shapes and sizes. You can win a scholarship for writing a prize essay, for example, but you can also win one by being in a special-interest group—for instance, an Armenian dental student in Ohio. Before you decide that you couldn't possibly win a scholarship, start looking around at all the available options.

You may be surprised to find that you are unique in several different ways that could spell scholarship winner for you.

—**based on information from** *The Ultimate Scholarship Guide 2010* **by Gen and Kelly Tanabe**

Best in Show: The Best Books to Help You Find and Get Scholarships

The Ultimate Scholarship Guide 2011 (published every year)

Gen and Kelly Tanabe have written an excellent resource for anyone looking for scholarships. Their listing of scholarships is good, but their advice about finding and pursuing scholarships is brilliant. From personal experience, they tell you exactly how to position yourself to win.

Buy this book. If you can't afford it, borrow it from your local library.

Scholarship Handbook 2011

The College Board has put together a really useful tool to find the right scholarships for you. There are 1.7 million students who win scholarship awards every year, and you can be one of them if you buy this book or borrow it from the library.

College Toolbox: Can You Recognize a Scholarship Scam?

With a difficult economy and the costs of tuition going up, students and parents alike are looking for more help to pay for college. Scholarships are one option, but the Federal Trade Commission (FTC) warns that some companies try to charge students for the same information they can access for free online. In general, if an offer looks too good to be true, it's probably a scam.

Unscrupulous businesses use lines such as those below to hook unwary students and their parents:

1. "We'll do all the work."

A company may be able to help you locate scholarships, but nobody can apply for those awards but you.

2. "The scholarship will cost money."

By definition, scholarships are "free money." You shouldn't have to pay to apply for them.

3. "You can't get this information anywhere else."

There are a number of free scholarship search services right on the web. Legitimate organizations that give out scholarships want the whole world to know about their award, so they won't keep it quiet or limit the information to a select few potential recipients.

4. "Results guaranteed or your money back."

No one can guarantee that you'll get a scholarship. In most cases, a board reads all the applications and then awards the money. No one knows how that board will vote ahead of time.

In addition, money-back guarantees are not to be trusted unless you are allowed to read the guarantee before you pay any money. Guarantees can be worded so that the company never has to give back a cent no matter what they do or promise to do.

5. "You have been selected to receive this scholarship" or you are a finalist for a scholarship that you never applied for.

Before you do anything else, check the web to be sure that the scholarship is legitimate. If you have any doubts at all, call your college's financial aid office or talk to your high school counselor to make sure that the scholarship exists.

6. "I need your credit card or checking account number to hold this scholarship."

Legitimate scholarships cannot be held for anyone. Don't give your financial information over the telephone unless you have contacted the organization yourself. Get the information in writing first. If you give a company your financial information, they may make a withdrawal from your account without your permission.

—based on information from the Federal Trade Commission website (www.ftc.gov)

ASK A LIBRARIAN

If you want to know everything about scholarships in your local area and worldwide, ask a librarian.

Librarians can help you find books, online materials, and databases of scholarship information along with insight into local organizations that might offer a scholarship to someone in the community.

Librarians are also handy to know when you want to understand how to win a scholarship competition and need samples of winning essays and applications to do that.

THE OUTSIDE SCHOLARSHIP AND YOUR FINANCIAL AID PACKAGE

While you may be reading this chapter just to figure out how to find, apply for, and win a scholarship, you also need to consider the ramifications of winning additional money for school.

An outside scholarship is a scholarship that does not come from the college itself. So, for example, if you win a $2,500 renewable scholarship award from your local newspaper, any college you apply to will consider this an outside award.

The financial aid office of your college has a great deal of leeway in handling this money. Some schools will use the scholarship to lessen any student loans in your financial aid package. Other schools use the scholarship to lessen any grants that you would have gotten from the college.

The salient point is that your college will SUBTRACT the outside scholarship monies from your financial aid package from the school. This doesn't mean that you shouldn't seek out scholarships. Scholarship money doesn't have to be paid back, so it's exactly the kind of financial aid that you want.

However, you need to talk to the financial aid office at your school (or look at the school's website) to figure out how the school deals with outside scholarships. If possible, you want the financial aid office to use the award instead of student loans. At worst, you want to know if the scholarship will replace other "free" money from grants in your financial aid package.

SCHOLARSHIPS

You may have wanted to skip this chapter because you believed that you weren't "special" enough to merit a scholarship. Luckily, you're here now because scholarships go to all different kinds of students for all kinds of reasons.

Every single unique fact about you could represent a scholarship opportunity. Think African American writer from upstate New York or daughter of a Filipino soldier majoring in law or comic book collector whose ancestors came over on the Mayflower. It's the combination of these things that make you scholarship-worthy.

There are certainly scholarships for those who get good grades and those who are gifted athletes or musicians, but there are also scholarships for people with an interesting ethnic background, those who are majoring in particular subjects or going into specific careers, and even those who hail from a particular region of the country or state in the union.

TIPS: *THE BIGGER THEY ARE*

DON'T FALL FOR THE "BIGGER IS BETTER" IDEA WHEN IT COMES TO SCHOLARSHIPS. SURE, $5,000 OR $10,000 FOR SCHOOL WOULD COME IN HANDY. HOWEVER, YOU CAN GET THAT SAME AMOUNT BY ZEROING IN ON SCHOLARSHIPS THAT **RENEW** EACH YEAR.

A $2,500-PER-YEAR SCHOLARSHIP CAN ADD UP TO $10,000 OVER THE COURSE OF YOUR STUDIES. AND THERE MAY BE FEWER STUDENTS VYING FOR THAT SMALLER SCHOLARSHIP, TOO.

—BASED ON INFORMATION FROM *THE ULTIMATE SCHOLARSHIP GUIDE 2010* BY **GEN AND KELLY TANABE**

For Instance: Unique Scholarships for Unique People

Mandy Scott's aunt, Patricia Cottinger, was determined that the girl get a scholarship to help her parents pay for college.

"I asked at the local library about scholarships for journalism students," Cottinger says. "I never thought there were scholarships specifically for gay students."

What Cottinger found was the Messenger-Anderson Journalist Scholarship and Internship Program. The Messenger-Anderson Program offers several $10,000 scholarships and internships to gay, lesbian, bisexual, and transgendered students who are studying journalism.

"Mandy's already filled out the application," Cottinger adds. "Now she's working on the essay. Next, we've got a mock interview planned. I want to give her every chance to win."

Personal Inventory

Start by filling out the College Personal Inventory at the end of this chapter. Answering all of the questions will assure you that you have left no stone unturned in order to get free money for school.

Remember, you may have to do a little digging (most of it online) to get a scholarship, but you don't have to pay the money back after graduation. Spending the time now is a better use of your time and your future earning potential.

Information about your parents and grandparents While it may not seem clear on the face of it, checking out the jobs, careers, professional organizations, volunteer activities, and hobbies of your parents and grandparents can yield big rewards in the scholarship category.

Many corporations have in-house foundations that give scholarships to the children and grandchildren of employees. In addition, most professional organizations (think International Association of Engineers or the Association of Realtors) also give scholarships. These can often be for those related to their members or for those going into the profession.

Also, volunteer community organizations such as the Kiwanis, Rotary, and Shriners do charitable work and often have nice big foundations of their own. That's why you want to quiz your relatives about what they belong to and who they know.

School and out-of-school activities

International knitters' guilds, comic book collectors organizations, and a whole host of other groups give scholarships based on hobby interests and school activities. Moreover, some scholarships are more interested in your out-of-school activities than your schoolwork because they value a well-rounded individual and will put their scholarship money where their beliefs are.

So, carefully consider all the questions, especially the ones that seem silly at the outset. You may be surprised about who gives scholarships and what they are looking for.

> ## *THE BOTTOM LINE ON SCHOLARSHIP SEARCH ENGINES*
>
> FinAid.org did some research about scholarship databases, and they judged FastWeb.com to be the biggest, the fastest, and the most accurate. (Full disclosure: FastWeb.com and FinAid.org are both part of the same corporate entity run by Mark Kantrowitz.)
>
> However, you may be surprised at the accuracy level of the other scholarship search engines and their speed. To find out everything you ever wanted to know on the subject, go to www.finaid.org/scholarships/awardcount.phtml#matchquality.

About the student Although some of the questions are personal (especially the ones about your sexual orientation and your religious beliefs), there are groups out there that give scholarships based on both of these facts. Answering the questions will help you to find scholarships that your classmates aren't qualified to apply for.

Where to Look for Scholarships

There are two ways to look for scholarships: online or off. The online method is much faster, but you will be working against pretty stiff competition. On the other hand, going old school may yield you the kind of unique scholarships that only you  (and maybe a handful of others) can qualify for.

Smart shoppers do both. Start with the easier online searching and then move along to the harder book search. Both can help you get the money you deserve.

Online scholarship searches Online scholarship searches are easy as long as you remember to completely fill in their query forms. If you leave something blank, there's less chance of finding a scholarship.

Of course, you could also just type in the word "scholarships" to your favorite search engine. However, that would produce hundreds of pages of entries. Instead, start with this list of the biggest and the best.

The following free scholarship search sites are listed in alphabetical order.

✦ College Board

The College Board has a nice big database that lists 2,300 sources of funding worth approximately $3 billion in aid at apps.collegeboard. com/cbsearch_ss/welcome.jsp. They also compile their own database.

✦ College View

College View has a large database that gets compiled quarterly at www.collegeview.com/financialaid/index.html.

✦ FastWeb.com

FastWeb has a huge database of scholarship information. You join for free, fill out the online form, and they'll e-mail potential scholarships to you. Nothing can be easier. Their hype says that they offer 1.5 million scholarships worth more than $3.4 billion. They are also always on the lookout for new scholarships. In fact, you can even apply online for some of awards they list at www.fastweb.com.

✦ Federal Government

For a Federal Student Aid Scholarship Search, go to this website: https://studentaid2.ed.gov/getmoney/scholarship/v3browse.asp.

✦ FindTuition.com

This site claims they have millions of awards worth billions of dollars in scholarship aid at www.findtuition.com/scholarships/.

✦ Military

If your parents, grandparents, or even your spouse are in the military, there could be a scholarship in your future. Check this website:

http://aid.military.com/scholarship/search-for-scholarships.do.

✦ Sallie Mae

Sallie Mae is a student loan company that also includes scholarship information at www.collegeanswer.com/paying/scholarship_search/ pay_scholarship_search.jsp.

✦ Scholarly Societies

Some academic and scholarly societies give scholarships to undergraduate and graduate students. Go to this website at the University of Waterloo Library to see what's available at www.scholarly-societies.org.

✦ Scholarships.com

This website says that it includes 2.7 million scholarships for a total of $19 billion dollars in aid at www.scholarships.com/.

✦ Specific major scholarships

Finaid.org includes a good selection of major-specific scholarships that you can search online at www.finaid.org/otheraid/majors.phtml.

✦ State Higher Education Agency Listings

Individual states have different scholarships and awards for students who live there. Find out what your state offers at http://wdcrobcolp01. ed.gov/Programs/EROD/org_list.cfm?category_ID=SHE.

Hitting the books While most scholarship-giving organizations will be on the web, there are a few holdouts that haven't gone mainstream. For them, you want to go old school and check the stacks.

However, you do not have to go it alone. Seek out the professionals below and ask for their help:

✦ Reference Librarians

Go to your local library and ask to speak to a reference librarian. Reference librarians are experts at ferreting out information that's kept in a book or database somewhere. They can help you find a book that lists organizations that award scholarships in your region, state, and locality. They may even know of some community organizations (such as the local Library Guild) that give scholarships.

✦ High School Counselors

Don't forget your high school counseling office. Go there and ask about scholarship books, flyers, websites—anything they have to offer.

✦ Local College Offices

Even if you don't plan to attend the college in town, you can find a great deal of information there. Go to the admissions and financial aid offices and ask about scholarships. Often, those at a college will hear about little-known scholarships available to local students even if they aren't going to the local college.

Telling everyone you know Networking is what most people do to get a job these days, but it will also work as a method to find scholarships. You are only one person. If you ask everyone you know and they ask everyone they know, soon you will be awash in scholarship information.

And don't forget about social media. If you put the word out on Facebook or Twitter that you want to know about scholarships, you'll be putting the best of the old school and the new school together for your own benefit.

It takes a village You're unique, so you probably won't be looking for the same types of scholarships as your friends. For this reason, you could create a study group for scholarships. You and one or two of your college-bound friends can help each other search for scholarships. Obviously, all the information you find about scholarships won't apply to you or your particular set of circumstances, but you would be able to help your friends and vice versa.

In addition, if your friends ask for help from everyone they know both online and off, you'll be creating a massive pool of people to help you. More people equals more information, which will likely equal more scholarships for all of you.

THE BASICS: TAXES AND YOUR SCHOLARSHIP

Some parts of your scholarship may be taxable. The general rule is that, if you are a student in a degree program, any scholarship money you get that pays for tuition and fees, books, required supplies, and equipment is not taxable. However, if you use some of your scholarship monies to pay for room and board or living expenses, that portion is taxable.

For more specific information, contact your accountant or tax professional or go to the IRS website (www.irs.gov) and print out a PDF copy of IRS Publication 970, "Tax Benefits for Education."

How to Apply for Scholarships

Most scholarships require at least an application form. Many require high school transcripts, letters of recommendation, and an essay from you. Be sure to check each scholarship website carefully to check the deadline and what is required to apply.

Applications Scholarship committees have their own form that you need to fill out. You can often download this from their website. However, you do occasionally have to write or call to get an application mailed to you.

High school transcripts You can show the scholarship organization your progress in school by sending your high school transcripts. But don't send them if they are not required for your application.

Essays Many scholarship groups will judge your worthiness for their award by reading an essay you've written on a subject chosen by the committee. In most cases, the essay requirement is not about quantity but about quality.

Make sure to finish your draft way ahead of schedule and have someone you trust help you edit it. Making friends with an English teacher could come in handy here.

Letters of recommendation Some scholarships require you to provide letters of recommendation from teachers and other nonfamily adults who know you well. Frequently, the organization will provide a form for this.

Because you will have to ask others to write letters for you, this requirement can eat up a great deal of time.

Deadlines Scholarship-giving organizations will not consider applications that come in late. In most cases, they will receive many more applications for aid than they could possibly award. For this reason, you need to follow every single requirement—especially the deadlines—to the letter.

The personal interview Few scholarships require a personal interview, but you need to be prepared in case you are a finalist for one of those. Like a job interview, you need to arrive neatly dressed, on time, and prepared to discuss your academic and personal interests coherently.

Fees You should not have to pay a fee to apply for a scholarship. If fees are required, you may want to look more closely at the scholarship to see if it's a scam. You can check with your local Better Business Bureau or the Federal Trade Commission (FTC) to file a complaint or check up on a scholarship organization.

Best in Show: The Best Websites For Winning Scholarships

The U.S. Department of Education has a nice micro website about how to find, apply for, and win scholarships.

http://studentaid.ed.gov/PORTALSWebApp/students/english/scholarships.jsp?tab=funding.

The College Board has some useful information about filling out applications and keeping track of your progress.

www.collegeboard.com/student/pay/scholarships-and-aid/8937.html.

FinAid.com has an excellent guide to winning a merit scholarship on their website.

www.finaid.org/scholarships/winning.phtml.

SCHOLARSHIP PERSONAL INVENTORY

Personal Characteristic	Student #1	Student #2	Student #3
Ancestry:			
Country where parents were born?			
County where grandparents were born?			
Ethnicity or Race: Arab, Black, Native American, etc.?			

Personal Characteristic	Student #1	Student #2	Student #3
Ancestors came over on the Mayflower? (Daughters of the American Revolution)			
Ancestors fought in the Civil War? (Daughters of the Confederacy)			
Female?			
Adopted?			
In Foster Care?			
Any racial minority?			
Mixed race?			
Religious Affiliation:			
Jewish, Catholic, Protestant, Buddhist?			
Parents?			
Grandparents?			
Student?			
Financial Need: (based on FAFSA data)			
Expected Family Contribution? (EFC)			
Recent financial issues such as parent losing job or house in foreclosure?			

Personal Characteristic	Student #1	Student #2	Student #3
Student is independent of parents?			
Parents and Grandparents: Jobs			
In politics?			
In military?			
Own small business?			
Parent or grandparent works for company with a foundation?			
Parent or grandparent belongs to a professional organization (i.e., ABA, Engineering Association, etc)?			
Parent or grandparent works in public service occupation (i.e., social worker, teacher, lawyer for low-income clients)?			
Parent or grandparent is doctor, lawyer, veterinarian, teacher?			
Parent or grandparent work for a union?			
Parents own a farm?			
Parent or grandparent is in police or firefighters?			
Parent or grandparent work for federal government?			

Personal Characteristic	Student #1	Student #2	Student #3
Parent or grandparent work for state government?			
Parents and Grandparents: Volunteer Work, Community Organizations, & Hobbies			
Rotary? Kiwanis? Shriners?			
Serve on the board of any not-for-profit organization?			
Fraternal orders such as Elks, etc.?			
Parents and Grandparents: Political Affiliation			
Republican?			
Democrat?			
Other?			
Student Information: School			
GPA?			
GPA in subject of college major?			
Extracurricular Activities?			
Team Sports?			
Non-Team Sports?			
Arts Activities (i.e., dance, writing, art, music)?			
Student Information: Outside School			
Volunteer Activities (i.e., nursing homes, animals, children)?			

Personal Characteristic	Student #1	Student #2	Student #3
Hobbies (i.e., sci-fi, making movies, knitting or crafts, collecting things, pets, reading, Irish dance, etc.)?			
Civic organizations such as Boy Scouts or Girl Scouts? Eagle Scout?			
Student Information: Jobs			
Does your company have a foundation (i.e., McDonald's or OfficeMax)?			
Did you ever work at a company with a foundation?			
Other?			
Student Information: Personal			
Sexual orientation or gender identity: gay, lesbian, trans-gender?			
Physical Impairments?			
Learning Disability?			
Political Affiliation?			
Religious Affiliation?			
Student Information: Talents			
Athletics (even if in school or outside school)			

Personal Characteristic	Student #1	Student #2	Student #3
Music (not in school) For example, have own band? Rapper? Ethnic musician?			
Writing (not in school) Poet? Screenwriter? Novelist?			
Art (not in school) Knitting, crochet Painting Drawing Cartooning Making movies Designing websites			
Dance (not in school) Ballet? Jazz? Modern? *So You Think You Can Dance* stuff?			
Student Information: College Major (can be tentative)			
Teaching?			
Law?			
Medicine?			
Engineering?			
Arts?			
Public Service (i.e., social worker, etc.)?			
Nontraditional career for your gender (i.e., engineering for women or nursing for men)?			
Other?			

Personal Characteristic	Student #1	Student #2	Student #3
Student Information: Colleges applied to for admission			
Does college have a foundation that gives scholarships?			
Location Information:			
State?			
County?			
City?			
Local major league sports teams (football, baseball, basketball)? Often, major teams have foundations.			
Local civic organizations— even if parents don't belong: (i.e., Soroptimists, Optimists, Odd Fellows, Elks, Rotary, Kiwanis, Shriners, etc.)			
Local teachers union?			
High school booster club?			
High school alumni group?			
PTA or parents' organization for high school?			
Local state representative?			
Local member of congress?			
Local newspaper?			
Local television station?			
Local radio station?			

Grants

❝ Any student who has ever received federal aid has Senator [Claiborne] Pell to thank for his or her education. The Pell Grants he created revolutionized our education system for generations of Americans who might not otherwise be able to pursue higher education.

—Senate Majority Leader Harry M. Reid, *Washington Post* **obituary for Senator Pell in 2009** **❞**

MYTH BUSTERS

Myth: I'm paying for college myself, so I don't need my parents' financial information.

Truth: Unless you are an independent student as defined by the Free Application for Federal Student Aid (FAFSA), the financial aid office at your school and the federal government will take your parents' income and assets into consideration when they figure out your financial aid package.

To see if you qualify as an independent student, go to www.fafsa .ed.gov.

**—from FAFSA frequently asked questions (FAQs)
at www.fafsa.ed.gov**

College Toolbox: Beware of Financial Aid Consultants

The world of financial aid can be confusing and a little scary. There are way too many acronyms and strangers peering at your tax information. However, the answer is not to hire your own financial aid consultant.

While there are certainly legitimate financial aid consultants out there, some are really just scam artists trying to find an easy mark. At best, a financial aid consultant will charge you for the same information that you can get for free from the financial aid office of your child's college.

At worst, a financial aid consultant can annoy or even hinder the administrators at your child's financial aid office. According to the College Board, all financial aid offices base their decisions on financial need and the aid formulas of their school to figure out the financial aid package for your child. You cannot bargain with them to get more aid and neither can your hired financial aid consultant.

—based on information from the College Board (www .collegeboard.com)

ASK A LIBRARIAN

If you think you already know everything there is to know about free money for school, think again.

Before you decide to give up on grants or scholarships, make a trip to your local library and talk to a reference librarian. Ask for help finding grants or scholarships to pay for school.

The reference librarian can point you toward databases, websites, books, and other resources that you never even considered.

The library should be your #1 source for information about how to pay for college and how to find free money for school.

GRANTS

Grants are different than scholarships. Scholarships are usually given for merit or because the applicant had all the qualifications the scholarship committee was looking for. A grant, on the other hand, is usually based on financial need. These need-based awards help low-income students to go to school.

Not surprisingly, the biggest awarder of grants is the federal government. One of the most well-known federal grants is the Pell. Millions of students have benefited from this award over the years (see the Pell box in this chapter). However, there are many other less well-known grants out there.

MYTH BUSTERS

Myth: I'm just trying to get admitted to college right now. I'll worry about financial aid once I'm admitted.

Truth: At colleges, financial aid is a scarce commodity. Even before you're accepted to a college, you need to fill out the Free Application for Federal Student Aid (FAFSA) online as close to January 1 as you can manage it.

Most colleges use the FAFSA to determine financial aid for students. You don't have to accept any or all of the financial aid that is offered, but none will be offered unless you fill out the FAFSA.

—from FAFSA frequently asked questions (FAQs)
at www.fafsa.ed.gov

Pell: The Most Famous Grant of All

The Pell Grant has been around since 1972. Named for Senator Claiborne Pell of Rhode Island, the program has helped 54 million low- and moderate-income students attend college, according to a *Washington Post* article in 2009.

As with most grants, the Pell is need-based. If your financial resources are slim, it's a good chance that you will be receiving a Pell grant to go to college.

As of the 2010–2011 school year, the maximum amount of Pell that a student can receive is $5,500 a year. The amount is calculated using the Expected Family Contribution (EFC) from the FAFSA information, the cost of attending your college, and a few other factors.

You are eligible to receive a Pell grant if you are:

✦ A U.S. citizen

✦ An eligible noncitizen

✦ Have a high school diploma

✦ Have a GED

✦ A student who has not earned a bachelors degree

One of the great advantages of the Pell is that your college can use it to pay for your room and board, your tuition, or your fees and then pay you directly anything that is left over. Some colleges pay students the Pell directly so that the student can pay for school.

Since the Pell is a government grant, you need to fill out the FAFSA to get it. As with all grants and scholarships, you are not required to pay them back after you graduate from college.

Personal Inventory

Most grants are need-based, but many are also slated for people in specific groups including race, ethnicity, and sex.

Use the Personal Inventory in the chapter on scholarships to help you zero in on grants for your particular situation. For example, if you are Jewish or Catholic, there may be need-based grants available to you based on these descriptors. On the other hand, if you are African American or Hispanic, there may also be need-based scholarships based on this factor.

Look at all the information about yourself and then look for need-based grants that include those factors.

Don't forget that the organizations that your parents and grandparents belong to may also provide need-based grants as well as scholarships to the children and grandchildren of their members.

Recognizing Grant Scams

The Office of the Inspector General of the Department of Education has issued a warning about a telephone grant scam that targets those looking for college financial aid.

The scam begins when someone calls claiming to be from the U.S. Department of Education. The person offers to change a student loan to an $8,000 grant but claims to need the student's bank information in order to charge a $249 processing fee to make the change.

The U.S. Department of Education does not call students or their parents and ask for bank information. In addition, there is no processing fee to apply for grants.

If you have been contacted by someone claiming to be from the U.S. Department of Education, report it to the OIC by calling their hotline number at 1-800-647-8733 or by e-mailing to oig.hotline@ed.gov.

According to the Office of the Inspector General, if you have given your bank or other financial information to these people, you need to do the following:

✦ Contact your bank right away. Tell the bank what happened. Ask the bank to close or monitor the checking account that was given over the phone.

✦ Alert the police about the incident.

✦ Report the crime to the OIG. Special agents with the OIG investigate these types of crimes.

✦ Contact the Federal Trade Commission (FTC) to report the crime at 1–877-FTC-HELP.

**—from the Office of Inspector General
of the U.S. Department of Education**

Where to Look for Grants

As with scholarships, there are two ways to search for grants: via books and via the Internet. You need to do both. Start with the easier online searching and then move along to the harder book search. Both can help you garner need-based support.

Online grant searches In this case, using your favorite Internet search engine can be helpful. But, instead of searching for "grants," be more specific about what you are looking for. Try "female, nontraditional college student grant" or "Hispanic accounting grant" or even "Native American female engineering college grant."

The goal is to not be too general or too specific. In one case, you'll find thousands of sites that you'll never be able to cull through, and in the other you'll be lucky to find one or two likely options.

Below are some places to get started organized by category.

✦ African American Student Grants

United Negro College Fund

www.uncf.org/ForStudents/index.asp

National Black Nurses Association

www.nbna.org/

✦ College Board

The College Board has a nice big database that includes grants as well as scholarships at http://apps.collegeboard.com/cbsearch_ss/welcome.jsp. They also compile their own database.

✦ Federal Government

You apply for federal grants such as the Pell Grant when you fill out the FAFSA. However, if you want to know more about government grants and all the grants programs available to you, go to the Ed.gov website:

www2.ed.gov/fund/grants-college.html?src=fp.

You can even get a forecast of the grants you are eligible for by using the Ed.gov FAFSA4caster at the Ed.gov website:

www.fafsa4caster.ed.gov/F4CApp/index/index.jsf.

Academic Competitiveness Grant (ACG)

www.studentaid.ed.gov/PORTALSWebApp/students/english/AcademicGrants.jsp?tab=funding

The National Science & Mathematics Access to Retain Talent Grant (National SMART Grant)

www.studentaid.ed.gov/PORTALSWebApp/students/english/SmartGrants.jsp?tab=funding

✦ Female Student Grants

American Association of University Women

www.aauw.org/learn/fellows_directory/index.cfm

The Educational Foundation for Women in Accounting

www.efwa.org/

✦ Hispanic Student Grants

Hispanic College Fund

www.hispanicfund.org/

National Association of Hispanic Nurses

www.thehispanicnurses.org/

✦ Minority Students

If you are African American, Hispanic, or Native American, you may be eligible for minority grants. Check out the listings at FinAid.org:

www.finaid.org/otheraid/minority.phtml

A Better Chance guide to college resources for students of color

http://abetterchance.org/abetterchance.aspx?pgID=1087

✦ Native American Grants

American Indian College Fund

www.collegefund.org/

Indian Affairs

www.bia.gov/index.htm

Hitting the books Not everything is online. For this reason, you will also want to look at grant directories in hard copy at the library.

Ask the following professionals to help you in your search for grants:

✦ Reference Librarians

Go to your local library and ask to speak to a reference librarian. Reference librarians are experts at ferreting out information that's kept in a book or database somewhere. They can help you find a book that lists organizations that award grants in your region, state, and locality.

✦ High School Counselors

Don't forget your high school counseling office. Go there and ask about grant books, flyers, websites—anything they have to offer.

✦ Local College Offices

Even if you don't plan to attend the college in town, you can find a great deal of information there. Go to the admissions and financial aid offices and ask about grants. Often, those at a college will hear about little-known grants available to local students even if they aren't going to the local college.

How to Apply for Grants

Unlike scholarships, each grant application is different. Since many grants are need-based, you will need to provide financial information about yourself and your family. Otherwise, some grants request an essay while others just want you to fill out an application.

However, like scholarships, grants have deadlines that are immutable. The money is limited, so, at the very least, you need to make the submission deadline to have a chance.

FAFSA Since the FAFSA is used by Pell and other grants from the federal government, it is also used by many grant-giving institutions. Go to the FAFSA website (www.fafsa.gov) to request that a copy of your Expected Family Contribution (EFC) and other financial materials are forwarded to the grant-giving organization.

Best in Show: The Best website For Grant Applications

The Foundation Center offers a free online webinar about how to approach foundations and win a grant for your education:

http://foundationcenter.org/getstarted/training/online/ product_online_training.jhtml;jsessionid=J4PFCCUBKX0P TLAQBQ4CGXD5AAAACI2F?id=prod2110005.

The Foundation Center also offers an online course in proposal writing to win grants:

http://foundationcenter.org/getstarted/tutorials/shortcourse/;jsessionid=J 4PFCCUBKX0PTLAQBQ4CGXD5AAAACI2F.

Grant and Scholarship Tracking Form

Keep track of all your grant and scholarship applications with this tracker. You can see at a glance what you still need to do and what the deadlines are.

GRANT AND SCHOLARSHIP TRACKING FORM

Action Taken	Grant A		Grant B		Scholarship A	
Sent application form(s)	X	Date		Date		Date
Sent FAFSA information (EFC)	X	Date		Date		Date
Sent transcripts		Date		Date		Date
Sent letter of recommendation #1		Date		Date		Date
Sent letter of recommendation #2		Date		Date		Date
Sent letter of recommendation #3		Date		Date		Date
Sent essay		Date		Date		Date
Scheduled in-person interview		Date		Date		Date
Misc.		Date		Date		Date
Misc.		Date		Date		Date
Misc.		Date		Date		Date

Jobs: On Campus, Off Campus, Internships, and Summer Jobs

> **"** I needed to work during college to help defray the costs of what my student loans and minimal Pell grants didn't cover. It helped put gas in the car, food and drink on the table, and if I was lucky, books in the bookshelf. In addition, it helped me socialize with non–college students, to remind me that there is something out there after school, more of a grounding in reality.
>
> **—Mike Welter, senior editor/producer, CNN "**

MYTH BUSTERS

Myth: I can't work while I'm going to college. It will hurt my grades.

Truth: Working too many hours while you are a college student may indeed hurt your grades. However, according to a recent study, working ten to twenty hours per week can actually help college students to be more organized with their school projects and eliminate the tendency to procrastinate.

The other advantages to working while you are in school are that you can borrow less on your student loans and show examples of real-world experience on your résumé.

—from a study sponsored by Upromise

AVOID JOB AND INTERNSHIP SCAMS

Be on the lookout for companies (both online and off) that try to charge you a fee for job and internship information that is already available for free on the Internet.

These bogus companies often "guarantee" that they can get you the exact job or internship that you want. Don't fall for it.

There are hundreds of free job boards online that charge employers for job listings and make those job listings free to job-seekers—including college students. (We've included the best of them in this chapter.)

If you are unsure about a company or an offer, go to the Better Business Bureau, the Federal Trade Commission, or Scam.com to see if the company has been reported.

Don't pay for information that is free on the Internet. And, don't get scammed.

—from http://scam.com

WANT A JOB ON CAMPUS?: LOOK FOR THE BUSIEST OFFICES

Looking for an on-campus job? Look for the busiest offices, and you could get hired.

Every office on campus hires student help. But the offices that are always busy, such as financial aid, admissions, accounting, and continuing education, need more help and the best workers.

If you can show that you're a student worker who will show up on time, do your work, and be flexible with your time, you could get hired on the spot.

So, look around for the busiest offices on campus and stop in to ask for a job. Don't be discouraged if the office you want has already hired all their student workers.

Drop by in two weeks or a month and ask again. Student workers come and go. And the office manager will be impressed that you cared enough about the job to come back.

If You Only Crack One Book This Summer: Try One of These

If you are looking for an adventure rather than just a stale summer job, this is the book for you: *The Back Door Guide to Short-Term Job Adventures: Internships, Extraordinary Experiences, Seasonal Jobs, Volunteering, Work Abroad.*

Author Michael Landes explains how to turn a simple job into an international adventure.

Of course, you can find this book and many others at your local library, including *Adventure Careers* by Alex Hiam and Susan Angle.

Although this book is written for a high school audience, it deals with finding a career and coming up with action plans to get you on your path. In addition, it advocates looking at both work and life in an entirely different way.

INTERNSHIPS

College Toolbox: The Top Five Questions to Ask About Your Internship

While most students can benefit from an internship, they aren't for everyone. Before you decide to look for an internship, make sure that it fits in with your major, your career goals, and your plans for the future.

To be sure, ask yourself the following five questions before seeking an internship:

1. How does this internship mesh with my career goals?

Sure, an internship at Disney World seems fun. What's not to like about California? But does it have anything to do with your major in engineering? While a summer job can be fun, an internship is supposed to give you real-world experience.

While you could certainly learn a great deal about how to run a business from working at a Disney resort, you may not learn much about engineering. So, choose an internship opportunity that fits with your career goals and not just your tanning regimen.

2. Is the internship paid or unpaid?

There's nothing wrong with an unpaid internship, but you need to be clear from the beginning about the kind of internship that you need. If money is tight, you may want to look for a paid internship before considering any unpaid opportunities.

Of course, if the perfect internship in you career field turns up, you may decide that the experience is worth more than the weekly wages.

3. Will this internship give me real-world experience?

Sad to say, some companies offer internships that include only grunt work. While filing and answering telephones is, indeed, real experience in the business world, it will probably not be useful in landing you a job after college.

Before you agree to anything, ask what the internship will include. Ask what work you'll be doing and who you will be working for. Good internship programs include a clear explanation of what you'll do and why it's helpful to your future career.

If possible, ask to speak to former interns, and query them about their experiences. That's the surest way to tell if the internship will be more than just busywork.

4. Will this internship give me experience in my field or career?

Although no internship is perfect, some will give you a better idea of the day-to-day life in your career than others. For example, if you're stuck filing plans away all day, you will hardly get an idea of what an architect's life is like on the job.

On the other hand, if you file plans for a few weeks and then go out on-site with the other architects or get to do some hands-on drafting, the internship will be a successful introduction to your future career.

Another consideration is if the internship may turn into a summer job or a job opportunity after college. Many companies choose employees based on internships, but ask about placement opportunities before you sign on.

5. Can I get college credit for this internship?

Even if you aren't getting paid, some internships can qualify for college credit. Check with your college and the internship program director to see what you need to do to get college credit for your work.

ASK A LIBRARIAN

Don't forget that your local librarian or the librarian at your college can help you find the perfect internship. From databases to websites to books, the nearest librarian has a treasure trove of information at his or her fingertips.

Don't be shy about asking for information about local, regional, or national internships or internships with well-known companies such as McDonald's, Disney, Coke, and others.

Your local librarian also knows where the jobs are, so ask where to find them.

JOBS

Working at a job while succeeding in college can take some organizational skills. However, the better you are at organizing your life in college, the better you will be at organizing your life after college.

In addition, getting some real-world work experience can make your résumé very inviting to future employers. Whether you decide to work during school, during the summer, or during an internship, this chapter will help you make the right choice for the job you want and help you to get the best possible job or internship at the best possible wage.

Types of Jobs

Although this chapter talks about different types of jobs, the truth is that many of these job types are not mutually exclusive and can overlap. For example, you might have a summer job that is an internship on campus. Or, you may have an on-campus job that has nothing to do with work study.

Whatever type of job you're looking for, this chapter will help you find it, land it, and take advantage of it.

On campus By definition, on-campus jobs are located somewhere within the confines of your college. This includes organizations that may be only loosely affiliated with your college such as research institutes, college bookstores, and not-for-profit organizations such as the college foundation.

On most campuses, the best way to find on-campus jobs is through the work study program at the financial aid office of your college. Work study is a method of financial aid that allows students to work during the school year. The financial aid money pays for the student's wages. Because of the financial aid money underpinning the system, most college offices prefer to hire work-study students because they have to pay only a small percentage of the student's wages from their budget.

However, this doesn't mean that you can't find an on-campus job if you don't have work study. Offices throughout your campus need student help, and they are happy to have student workers they can count on.

Off Campus Off-campus jobs are, of course, those jobs outside the college. Sometimes these jobs include fast food restaurants and other service businesses, but they can also include small businesses around the campus and even online businesses that you could work for virtually from the comfort of your dorm room or apartment.

Summer The beauty of summer jobs is that you might be able to work for the same office or company that you work for during the school year. College offices still need help during the summer break, and businesses frequently need help gearing up for the busy season.

Another option, however, is for you to work at home during the summer holidays or even to work somewhere entirely different. If you already have a job squared away in your hometown, it makes sense to go back to it every summer. But, if you have to find a new job every summer, you may want to consider the opportunities available from major resort operators, such as Disney, to travel and get college credit while you're working with other college students from around the country. You don't even have to sing or dance to get a job—but it helps.

Internship Like summer jobs, internships are limited-time jobs that you work for money, for credit, or for the fun of it. If you aren't getting paid, you often earn college credit for your time. Whether you are paid or not, you do earn real-world work experience and also a list of people that you can use for professional references when you finish college.

In addition, your internship may turn into a summer job or even a full-time job once you have graduated.

Volunteering Although you won't be paid for volunteering, you will earn real-world experience and be able to list this experience on your résumé. You will also find people you can use as professional references when you finish college, and you might even find a job after you graduate.

FOR INSTANCE: START YOUR OWN COMPANY

Malla Duffy was tired of saying, "Do you want fries with that?" but she couldn't find a better job. Instead of giving up, Malla created her own job.

"My grandfather ran his own business until he retired and my Dad took over," she says. "I figured that I could do the same thing using the Internet."

She took inspiration from what she liked to do: knit and crochet.

Today, Malla designs knitting patterns and sells them in her virtual store at etsy.com. She also sells her designs to knitting magazines such as Knitty.com and *Interweave Knits*.

"I'm having fun, learning new things all the time, and I'm making enough to pay for room and board," Malla adds. "And I can work from home or my dorm room."

—based on information from www.finaid.org

Before You Apply: Things to Take into Consideration

Getting a job may seem pretty easy. However, your future employer will have a variety of questions to ask you about your past work experience and your availability.

You can be sure to know all the answers in advance if you take a few minutes to consider the following questions before you look for a job:

Where do you want to work? Do you have a preference about where you work? Do you hate fast food restaurants? Do you have a background in cooking? Do you know everything there is to know about computers?

Think about where you want to work and where you don't want to work. This will help you narrow the field of possible jobs.

Also, consider the geographical location. Do you want to work in your hometown during the summer or go off to Idaho and work as a volunteer? Do you love to hike and participate in outdoor activities? Maybe there's a camp job in your future.

When do you want the job? When do you need the job? Are you looking for a summer gig when it's just November? Are you looking for an internship that's a year away?

Think about when you want the job, so you can start looking well in advance.

How many months can you work? How long do you plan to work at this job? Are you planning to work for just a semester or the whole school year? Are you looking for just a month's work in the summer or will you try to work part-time during the school year, as well?

Your employer will want to know exactly how long you plan to work.

Internship Dos and Don'ts

In difficult economic times, you need to set yourself apart from others who are applying for jobs. You can do that by completing one or more internships while you are in school.

The advantages of internships are that you get real work experience that you can use on your résumé after you get out of school, and you make friends with people who can help you get a job after college. These people can become your business network as you move through your career.

However, you need to remember that the work environment is very different from being in school. For this reason, QuintCareers.com created an e-book about finding and landing an internship.

Their top ten list of dos and don'ts include the following:

1. Do act professionally at all times, and expect to be treated professionally in turn.
2. Do try to meet on a regular basis with the supervisor of your internship.
3. Don't be afraid to ask questions. That's what an internship is all about.
4. Do meet as many people from the company as you can.

5. Do any and all work that is asked of you, including the boring filing or copying.

6. Do keep in touch with your coworkers when you go back to school.

7. Don't engage in office politics or gossip.

8. Do send thank-you notes to the people you worked with during your internship.

9. Do end on a high note. Don't complain in the exit interview.

10. Do get another internship so that you can gain more experience.

You can read all eight chapters of *The Quintessential Guide to Finding and Maximizing Internships* from QuintCareers.com at the following URL:

www.quintcareers.com/Quintessential_Careers_Press/Internship_Guide/.

How many hours a week can you work? One of the first questions you will be asked in any job interview is how many hours you can work in a week. You can save yourself countless headaches by thinking about that right from the beginning.

If you try to work too many hours during school, you may hurt your grades. By the same token, if you work only part-time during the summer, you may not make enough money to pay for your books or materials for school.

So, how many hours do you think you can work?

What do you want to be paid? If you're only after minimum wage, you probably won't have any trouble finding a job. However, you may want to think about how much you can make over the summer, per week, or per month, especially if you're working during the school year and using the money to pay for school fees.

What are your skills? Have you had a job before? What did you do? What did you learn? Do you have skills that could translate into a job such as computer skills or experience working a cash register? Have you worked in fast food or in retail?

Make a list of your former jobs and the skills you learned. If you haven't worked before, make a list of your skills. Don't discount skills such as politely answering the telephone or filing. Those job skills would make you a perfect receptionist or file clerk.

Where to Look for Jobs

You can find jobs all around you at college and at home. All you have to do is open your eyes and look for opportunities. In addition, the Internet has all kinds of options to find a job or work a virtual job.

Your college Almost every location at your college can hide tips and hints about jobs in the area. Look around, especially at bulletin boards, to see what's available.

✦ Financial Aid Office

Many financial aid offices have listings of current jobs on the bulletin boards, in a newsletter, or online.

✦ Employment/Jobs Office

Most colleges have an employment, recruitment, or jobs office on campus. Go there and search for local or regional jobs or just jobs on campus.

✦ College website

Your college probably has a website, so go there and look for jobs. Some on-campus jobs will be listed, but many colleges also include student jobs on their job board.

✦ Bulletin Boards

At college campuses, jobs are often posted on bulletin boards around campus. While you're waiting to get into your classroom or talking with friends, peruse the nearest bulletin board, and see if there are any jobs you're interested in.

✦ Busiest Campus Offices

As noted earlier, the busiest college offices usually hire the most student workers. If you see a long line of students, that's the place where you want to apply for a job.

✦ Dorm—RA, food service, night porter

Don't forget that your dorm is also a part of the campus. Dorms almost always have jobs for Resident Assistants (RAs), for food service jobs, and for jobs watching the doors at night, sometimes called the night porter or night guard.

Your college town Your college town is also full of jobs if you know what to look for.

✦ Want Ads

Start with the paper want ads in the student newspaper and then move on to the local town paper. If they have an online version, look up the jobs there.

✦ Businesses Near Campus

Look at the businesses near campus and see if any of them are hiring. Most campuses have bookstores, copy centers, and fast food restaurants in close proximity to the student population. All of those places need workers.

✦ Bookstores

If you can't get a job at the campus bookstore, try a bookstore in town or close to campus. Bookstores are generally good places to work, and you can often get discounts on books.

✦ Townie Businesses

If you live off campus, look around for businesses near where you live. Most businesses not near the campus will also be interested in hiring college student labor. You can always walk in and ask the owner.

DON'T FORGET: TEMP AGENCIES AND SMALL BUSINESSES

While you're thinking about summer jobs—in your hometown or in your college town—don't forget the local temporary agencies. They can find you one job for the summer or a variety of jobs.

If you've got any experience with computers, filing, or telephones, you can probably find a good temp job for the summer . . . and maybe for the school year.

In addition, don't forget about small businesses in your college town or hometown. While small businesses don't usually have the funds to take out a big advertisement, they often have jobs in the summer.

The best way to find these jobs is to stop by the company and ask. You may just be able to create your own job on the spot.

**—based on information from
Trinity College in Hartford, CT
www.trincoll.edu/depts/career/guides/summer_job.shtml**

Online There are hundreds of job boards on the Internet, but here are the best ones for college students, summer jobs, volunteer opportunities, and internships.

✦ Summer Jobs

While you can still find a full-time job here, Monster.com is still the biggest and the best online source for part-time or seasonal jobs.

www.monster.com

If you want to work on a cruise ship or at a resort or camp, this may be the site for you. Registration is free, and they include a complete list of the job titles and job responsibilities for cruise ship personnel.

www.a+summerjobs.com

If you don't mind working hard, you could be a college painter. Each year, this company trains students to be entrepreneurs by painting houses and cleaning windows. You can sign on just to paint or to move up in the leadership food chain.

www1.collegepro.com/sb.cn

This website, published by the local consortium of California libraries, includes lots of local jobs in California along with loads of useful information about writing a résumé, creating a cover letter, and figuring out your career path.

www.jobstar.org

If you'd like to work at a camp or a national park, this is the site for you. The jobs include resorts, theme parks, ski resorts, ranches, and tour companies.

www.coolworks.com

If you want to work overseas, this is the job site for you. Whether you want to tend bar in Europe or pick fruit in New Zealand, this is the place.

www.summer-jobs.com

This is the must-have site for those looking for an hourly gig. You can search by state, and their employers include big-name companies like ATT and Halloween USA.

www.snagajob.com

This site lists full-time, seasonal, and internship jobs for younger workers that include the likes of MTV, Amnesty International, and Apple, as well as fascinating day-in-the-life articles about all kinds of people in all kinds of jobs.

www.getthatgig.com

This site has been offering summer jobs for a decade, and their target audience is high school and college students and new college grads.

www.summerjobs.com/

If you want to work at a Disney resort or work in Alaska, this is the resort job site for you. They're hooked into a number of major resorts, and they offer advice about how to land the jobs.

www.resortjobs.com

✦ Camp Jobs

This site lists 167 camps looking for staff. You can also list your résumé for free.

www.campstaff.com/

Use this site to search by state, country, or position you want. You can also list your résumé here for camp owners to see.

www.campjobs.com/

This site makes it easy to find jobs at residential camps. You send in your résumé, and the site sends it directly to all the camps that subscribe. Interested camps can then call or e-mail you.

www.mysummers.com/default.aspx

✦ Internships

This site offers internships with the likes of Deloitte, Google, Nestlé, and Enterprise. You need to register (it's free) to see their listings.

www.interninc.com/

InternWeb.com offers free sign-up for students seeking internships.

www.internweb.com/

This website run by AboutJobs.com includes internships from NBC/Universal, the U.S. Department of State, and Disney. Signing up is free for internship seekers.

www.internjobs.com/

✦ Volunteering

If you want to volunteer at a national park, you can find out everything you need to know at this website for the National Park Service (NPS).

www.nps.gov/getinvolved/volunteer.htm.

You can also volunteer to help in your own community or across the nation at www.serve.gov. You can even create your own volunteer project and list it on this site.

www.serve.gov/.

Your hometown If you want to get a summer job at home, use the want ads in your local paper or go online to see what's available.

Don't forget that you can also just walk into a business and ask about jobs. You may find a position that hasn't even been advertised yet.

Your family Use your family to help you network to find a job. If your parents own a business, you can work for them during the summer.

If your parents have friends with businesses, maybe you can work for a friend over the summer, or your parents may know someone who hires college students.

Don't be afraid to ask everyone you know, including great-aunts and uncles and cousins, if they know of any jobs for the summer.

Your friends Ask your friends where they are working for the summer and see if you can get an interview for that company. Ask them to help you network to find a summer job.

Virtual jobs The Internet could provide a job for you if you have a laptop or desktop computer. Some companies are happy to hire virtual workers who can work from anywhere.

✦ Demand Studios

This online portal hires writers and editors. If you qualify, you can work at your own pace on the articles of your choice. They pay via PayPal, too.

www.demandstudios.com/

Your local temp agency may also have spaces available for virtual assistants, web designers, and web programmers. Check to see if you can work at home during the summer.

Start your own business If your local temp agency doesn't offer jobs for virtual assistants, web programmers, or web designers, and you have the skills, you could start your own business.

You could also mow lawns, babysit, or tutor children. If you can't find a job, maybe it's time to create your own job.

What You Need to Succeed in Your Job Hunt

You need three things to succeed in getting a job: a résumé, a cover letter, and some skill at interviewing.

Here's an overview of each item:

Résumé A résumé is nothing more than a one- or two-page summary of your work experience. However, it can be a little overwhelming to write your very first one. For this reason, you might consider going to your local library and asking the librarian to help you find a book with step-by-step instructions.

Also, be ready to write more than one version of your résumé. For example, if you have had jobs at camp and in an office, you would want to create one résumé for each type of experience.

In addition to books, you might try these websites that offer articles, advice, and sample résumés for you to look at:

+ www.ehow.com/first-resume/

eHow has a variety of articles that will walk you through the résumé-writing process. This link is especially for those writing their first résumé.

+ www.internweb.com/articles/

InternWeb.com has a variety of articles about creating a résumé to land an internship, but those same tips can also help you land a job.

Cover letter Cover letters can be tricky. First, a definition. The cover letter is the piece that goes along with the résumé. A cover letter is supposed to succinctly list the job skills on your résumé that relate to the position you want.

Cover letters are short—just one page. However, as with résumés, you may want to write several versions to use for different types of jobs.

Of course, there are books on this topic, too. Here are a couple of websites that have sample cover letters and can walk you through the process of creating your own cover letter.

+ www.aftercollege.com/content/career_resources/e/cover_
   letters_an_endangered_species/

This article explains exactly why cover letters are important even in the age of the Internet.

✦ www.collegecentral.com/ArticleList.cfm?CatID=CAR

College Central has a variety of articles to help you write the perfect cover letter for every job opportunity.

Interviewing 101

Your résumé and cover letter will get your foot in the door, but your interview will really get you the job. Be prepared for everything that the interviewer will ask by following these tips from the Bureau of Labor Statistics.

Preparation You can prepare for the interview by learning about the organization. Find the company's website online and read all about them. Be prepared to answer general questions about your previous job experience and why you want the current job.

The interviewer may begin with very broad questions such as "Tell me about yourself," or "What are your strengths and weaknesses?" Think about how you plan to answer these questions in advance. If possible, practice answering these types of interview questions with a friend.

Personal appearance Be neat and clean, even if you are wearing blue jeans and a t-shirt. If the job is in an office, dress appropriately for an office. If you err, err on the conservative side. Don't wear frayed clothing or anything that shows too much skin. In addition, don't wear too much makeup, jewelry, or cologne.

The interview Arrive early for the interview. Be prepared to speak clearly and don't use slang. Bring a list of questions that you want to ask about the company or the job. Unless the interviewer brings it up, don't ask about salary.

Be polite with everyone. Make eye contact with the interviewer and sit up straight. Shake hands with the interviewer at the beginning of the interview and at the end. Remember to thank the interviewer after the interview.

What to bring to the interview Here's a list of items to bring with you to the interview:

+ Social Security card
+ Driver's license
+ Résumé
+ Application (if required)
+ References (Most employers ask for the names and contact information for three references.)
+ Transcripts (These are not always necessary, but it's a good idea to bring them anyway. It shows the interviewer that you are prepared.)

After the interview When you get home from the interview, send a short thank-you note to the person who interviewed you. Explain that you are even more interested in the job after the interview.

Best in Show: The Best Websites for Résumés, Cover Letters, and Interview Tips

Monster College has everything to help the new college graduate find a job, but they also have a great deal of information about internships, writing résumés, and interviewing.

http://college.monster.com/training/articles/2-what-is-monstercollege

JobStar.org has some excellent résumé tips as well as a good listing of sample résumés. They've also got a good sampling of cover letters.

http://jobstar.org/index.php

Worktree.com has articles about résumés, cover letters, and interviewing, including samples of what to do and what not to do. They also have a variety of general tips about how to be successful on the job.

www.worktree.com/index.cfm

The Bureau of Labor Statistics (BLS) has tips about applying and interviewing for jobs.

www.bls.gov/oco/oc020045.htm

DON'T PAY FOR A RÉSUMÉ OR COVER LETTER

While it might seem like a good idea to pay someone else to write your résumé and cover letter, you will only be hurting yourself.

Learning to write both a résumé and a cover letter is an integral part of being a working adult. If you shirk now, how will you ever learn to write a résumé?

Will you pay someone every single time that you write or rewrite your résumé? That could add up to a huge expense.

I know, I know. Those résumé-writing services make it sound as if they have the special magic mojo to get you the job of your dreams. As with any and all scams, you don't want to pay for something that you can easily do for yourself.

So, don't pay someone else to write your cover letter or résumé. Who knows your job skills better than you do?

JOB/INTERNSHIP COMPARISON WORKSHEET

	Job #1	Job #2	Job #3
Name of company			
Name of manager			
Job location			
Job pay per hour			
Job daily hours			
Length of job in months			
Job activities			
Job benefits?			
How get to job each day: bus, car, walk?			
How heard about job?			

Loans

> 66 It's cheaper to save than to borrow. If you borrow instead of saving, you will pay twice as much. When you save, you get the interest, but when you borrow, you pay the interest.
> **—Mark Kantrowitz, publisher of www.finaid.org and www.fastweb.com** 99

MYTH BUSTERS

Myth: I can just borrow what I need to pay for college. I'll easily be able to pay it back after I graduate.

Truth: When institutions are offering you money, it's tempting to just say YES. After all, once you pay for school, you can use some of that leftover loot to buy a new computer or additional software. Hey, that's a school supply, right?

However, you have to pay loans back with interest, so be careful about what you will and will not accept.

There is a hierarchy to aid. Take the "free" aid first—that is, aid that you don't have to pay back, such as scholarships, grants, and work study.

After exhausting all of those options and discussing it with your family, consider federal student loans next because they're usually the cheapest option. Finally, look at student loans that are not guaranteed by the Feds.

Factoid: Loans Are a Fact of Life for College Students

According to the College Board, 50 percent of undergraduates apply for and accept at least one student loan to pay for their education.

Best in Show: The Best Loan Comparison Calculators

Make sure that you're getting the best deal on loans by using these calculators from the College Board.

This calculator will compare loans to make sure that you're getting the best deal. You can look at the terms of each loan including the overall costs and length of repayment.

http://apps.collegeboard.com/loancompare/ loancomparison.doc

This calculator can help you compare the terms of private/alternative loans. In general, loans that are not subsidized by the federal government will cost you more.

http://apps.collegeboard.com/loancompare/loancomparisonintro.jsp

FIVE TIPS ABOUT BORROWING MONEY

Most students have never borrowed money before they go to college and face the prospect of a student loan to pay for their education. Be a smart consumer and prepare yourself by following these five tips.

#1: Compare rates and shop around.

Your college's financial aid office and even your local bank can offer you suggestions about where to get a student loan, but it's your job to compare the interest rates, the repayment schedule, and the other terms of the loan. Don't be afraid to ask if they can make you a better deal. Although it isn't exactly like shopping for a car, the idea of talking to a variety of lenders to get the best possible deal does apply.

#2: Meet all the deadlines.

When you get the award letters from the schools you have applied to, you need to make careful note of the due dates. If you are going to accept the financial aid and attend that school, you need to make sure that the school knows this as soon as possible. If you will not be attending a school, alert them as soon as you can because they will award the financial aid to someone else. You don't want your financial aid package to go to someone else because you missed the deadline by a day or two.

#3: Take only what you need.

Although it seems like "free" money, it's not. Borrow only what you think you'll need for one year of school. You can always go back and borrow more if you need it. Letters from the financial aid office are only offers. You are not required to take everything there. It's not an all-or-none proposition. You can decide to accept the grants and scholarships but decline the student loans.

#4: Ask about fees.

Make sure you ask about any fees that will be required to prepare the loan. The fees are usually taken right off the top of the loan itself, which will leave you with slightly less money than you expected. Ask to have the fees explained, so you know what they are for and exactly how much of the loan you will receive.

#5: Make interest payments on unsubsidized student loans.

You can save yourself a great deal of money if you can pay the interest on your unsubsidized student loan while you're a student. The cost to you at the time will be minimal, but you can save yourself thousands by the time you have to pay the loan back.

ASK A LIBRARIAN

Whether you want to know the best place in your community to get a student loan or the easiest method to research loans online, go to your local library.

Librarians can help you find books, CDs, DVDs, websites, and databases with all the information you need to make good decisions about taking out a loan.

LOANS: WHAT TO LOOK FOR

When you look at the various loans that
you are offered, you want to consider
just a few important points:

+ Interest rate: This is how much
  you will be paying every year for
  the privilege of borrowing the money. Lower is always better.

+ Subsidized: A subsidized loan means that the federal government will be paying the interest while you are in school. That
  will save you money.

+ Credit check: Loans from the federal government don't have
  credit checks. They are need-based and backed by the government itself. However, loans from private sources such as banks
  require a credit check. Since most students don't have much of a
  credit record yet, banks require students to get a cosigner, usually
  the student's parents. If the student cannot pay the loan back and
  defaults, the parents would be responsible to pay back the loan.

+ Borrower: Who will be the borrower on the loan? Many loans
  are made to students. However, some loans are made to parents
  or to students with their parents as cosigners. Having a cosigner
  means that your parents would be responsible to pay the loan
  back if you could not pay.

+ Repayment schedule: Most federal student loans are meant to be
  paid back in the ten years after you graduate from college. For
  those going to medical school, graduate school, or law school,
  that time period is often extended to twenty five years.

GETTING LOANS TO PAY FOR COLLEGE

Loans should be your last stop on the road to financial aid. Luckily,
most colleges put together a financial aid package, with all the aid from
the college and the information from filling out the FAFSA, which
includes work study, grants, many scholarships, and student loans.

You can view a sample financial aid letter compliments of the U.S. Department of Education at their Student Aid on the website (https://studentaid2.ed.gov/getmoney/pay_for_college/award.html). They also offer an award worksheet to help you figure out exactly what your award letter means and a comparison worksheet to compare awards from different schools.

The important thing to remember about your financial aid package is that you don't have to accept it. If, for example, your top choice school offers you $3000 in work-study money, $5,000 in grants, and $15,000 in student loans, you can agree to accept everything except the loan.

Sadly, the FAFSA and the financial aid office at your school determine which of the federal programs you may participate in and even how much you may receive as a loan from each program. This is based on the EFC (Expected Family Contribution), which is based on the financial information that you included in your FAFSA application.

However, there are several federal programs and dozens of private lenders that you can choose from if you and your family need extra funds to pay for school.

The Five Types of Loans

There are four types of federal student loans for undergraduates and one type of private loan. Each type of loan has different requirements including interest rates, repayment options, and who may borrow the money. For an overview of all the loans including how much may be borrowed each year, look at the chart at the end of this chapter.

Perkins If you qualify for a Perkins loan, it is almost always a good idea to take it because this loan is subsidized, and the interest rate is just 5 percent and fixed.

The Perkins loan is need-based. Students are the borrowers. The funds are only available to students with a greater financial need. This means that you can only apply for a Perkins loan if the financial aid office at your school tells you that you can in your award letter.

In addition, this loan is subsidized. A subsidized loan is one where the federal government pays the interest while you are in school and often continues to pay the interest until six months after you have graduated from college. A subsidized loan is cheaper because the interest has been paid. For many student loans, the interest is added to the principal which means that you are borrowing more and will therefore have more to pay back. Always choose a subsidized loan over an unsubsidized one.

The interest rate is just 5 percent and is fixed for the life of the loan. Many private loans have variable interest rates that can go up during the loan period.

Subsidized stafford The subsidized Stafford loan is also based on the financial needs of the student. After July 2010, the interest rate on this loan is just 4.5 percent a year. As with the Perkins loan, you can only get this loan if the financial aid office at your school says that you can. You qualify based on your FAFSA information including the EFC. But if you qualify, this is a very advantageous loan to get.

DEBT: UNDERSTANDING YOUR LIMITS

Financial experts suggest that you stop and think before you take on too much debt, especially student loans. Since it can take anywhere from ten to twenty five years to pay off all your student loans, it pays to think carefully before you sign on the dotted line.

In general, parents are advised to make sure that their total debt is no more than 37 percent of the family's gross income.

For students, the amount of monthly student loan payments should be lower—no more than 15 percent of the student's income.

Unsubsidized stafford The unsubsidized Stafford (as the name implies) requires that you pay the interest even while you are in college. However, most students agree in the beginning to add the interest to the principal. This is called capitalizing the interest, and it will cause you to pay more in the long run. If at all possible, you should try to pay the interest instead of capitalizing, it because you'll be required to pay back less at the end of the loan.

The advantage of this loan is that it is not based on financial need, so it can be used to pay your family's share of your college expenses.

The rate is just 6.8 percent and fixed for the life of the loan. However, this loan works in conjunction with its subsidized sibling, so you have to subtract the subsidized amount from the unsubsidized.

Parent PLUS The federal government does sponsor one loan program that loans money to the parents of students going to college. That's the Parent PLUS loan. The interest rate is fixed at 7.9 percent. The only disadvantage to this loan is that parents can borrow up to the entire cost of their children's education, but they must first subtract any financial aid that their children are getting.

Private loans (alternative, state, and others) If you are not eligible for the federal student loans or if your college costs will be more than your financial aid offer, you can apply for a private loan. Private loans can come from your local bank, your state, the foundation at your college, your college, or even a separate organization such as the aid society for the Air Force, Marines, Army, or Navy.

The rates will be higher than the federal loans, and you will be required to pay the interest while you are in school or capitalize it. In addition, the interest rate may be variable, which means that it could go up while you are in school. Then you would have to pay back even more than you expected when you signed the loan papers.

Moreover, private loans also do a credit check. Most students need a cosigner who is almost always the parents. However, if your parents do not have a good credit record, you may not be able to get a private loan at all.

How The Loan Process Works

As covered in the chapter on financial aid, when you apply for admission to a variety of colleges, you also send your FAFSA information to those schools. You may also be asked to fill out additional forms that each school may have for financial aid including grants, scholarships, and work study.

When the school agrees to admit you, they also send you a financial aid letter. This letter is really just a suggestion about how you and your family can pay for school. You do not have to accept the whole package. You can choose to accept the work study, the grants, and the other gift aid that you are not required to pay back, and you may decide not to accept the student loan offer.

On the other hand, you may decide that a federal subsidized loan is a good option for you and your family. If you agree to accept everything in the financial aid letter, you usually need to sign the letter, date it, and mail it back to the financial aid office by a specific deadline.

The deadline is in place because any financial aid that you decline will be offered to another student. By this same token, if you do not sign the letter or get it to the financial aid office by the deadline, you may not be eligible for any of the awards.

Any federal student loans that you are offered will be on the letter. Once you sign and return that letter, the financial aid office at your school will help you fill out the rest of the paperwork, which will include a promissory note. This note spells out the student loan amount, the subsidized or unsubsidized nature of the loan, the interest rate, the repayment plan, and everything else you need to know about the loan.

In most cases, the financial aid office of your school will take the loan amount to pay for your school fees, room and board, and tuition. Any money leftover for your living expenses is usually paid to you by check from the financial aid office. This is called a disbursement, and it may happen once or twice a year, depending on the schedule of your school.

Finding a Loan

If you have to take out a private loan, there are a variety of places that you can look for one, including the following:

Your local bank If you have a checking and savings account at a bank, that bank may be willing to lend you money for college. Go in and check with a banking executive.

Your parents' bank If your parents have a small business or have been doing business with the same bank for a number of years, you may want to talk with the bank manager or another executive about a student loan.

Online

+ Finaid.org has a big list of lenders for student loans on their website. (www.finaid.org/loans/educationlenders.phtml).

+ The College Board includes student loans in their scholarship search engine. (http://apps.collegeboard.com/cbsearch_ss/welcome.jsp)

+ Military.com has a listing of scholarships, grants, and loans for those in the military community including veterans, spouses, and children of soldiers. (http://aid.military.com/scholarship/search-for-scholarships.do)

+ Sallie Mae offers student loans along with 529 savings plans. (www.salliemae.com/)

SAY WHAT?: Loan Terms Explained

Like the financial aid office, banks and other lenders for student loans have their own vocabulary. Since you need to know what they mean so you can make sense of the paperwork before you sign on the dotted line, here's the skinny on the most common terms:

+ Cancellation: Loan cancellation is when the bank cancels the loan. Some governmental programs (such as the Peace Corps) will cancel all or part of your student loans in exchange for your service.

+ Capitalizing the loan: This means that you add the yearly interest to the principal of the loan. Obviously, a capitalized loan will cost you more to pay back.

+ Deferment: Deferment is when the bank allows you to put your monthly payments on hold. Some banks will do this if you are in graduate school or involved in a government program of service.

+ Disbursement: This is the check that your financial aid office will give to you once or twice a year. Usually, this is any money leftover from a student loan once your fees, room and board, and tuition have been paid.

+ Forbearance: Forbearance is when the bank allows you to stop making monthly payments for a short time because you are having financial difficulties.

+ Loan consolidation: Loan consolidation is when the bank puts all of your student loans together into one bigger loan. The advantage is that you have longer to pay it off. The disadvantage is that your total cost will be higher.

+ Need-based: This means that the loan is based on the financial need of the student as determined by the FAFSA.

+ Subsidized: Subsidized means that the federal government pays the interest rate on the student loan until the student graduates from college or is not enrolled at least half time as a student.

STUDENT LOANS AND TAXES

Parents can deduct the interest payments on loans they take out for the education of their children on their taxes. In general, the deduction is $2,500 per year for the life of the loan, but some restrictions apply. Students can take the same deduction.

Read IRS Publication 970 (Tax Benefits for Education) to get all the information at www.irs.gov/publications/p970/index.html.

Repaying Student Loans

The good news is that paying back your student loan just got easier. The Feds finally got the message that new college graduates don't make big bucks at their first jobs. For this reason, the federal government has instituted two new programs that should make it much easier for new college grads to make their loan payments.

In addition, the feds also have a plan in place to forgive whatever you owe after twenty five years, or just ten years if you work in public service sector jobs.

Income-based repayment The first program, called Income-Based Repayment (IBR), is just what it sounds like. Instead of basing your monthly payments on what you owe, this program bases the payment on what you actually make in your new job (assuming you have one).

For more information about this option, go to the IBR website at www.ibrinfo.org, or go to the U.S. Department of Education's website for a question-and-answer document that explains all the changes and when they become available.

Public service loan forgiveness The second program, called Public Service Loan Forgiveness (PSLF), offers loan forgiveness for those who work in particular public service jobs such as teaching in a low-income neighborhood, practicing law as a public defender, or being a doctor in a rural community.

For more information about how exactly you can get all or part of your student loan forgiven, go to the U.S. Department of Education's student aid on the web portal at http://studentaid.ed.gov/PORTALS-WebApp/students/english/PSF.jsp.

LOAN FORGIVENESS FOR THE REST OF US

If you don't work in a public service sector job, you can still get some or all of your student loan debt forgiven. If you join the military, the Peace Corps, or other volunteer groups, you can gain student loan forgiveness. Even some government jobs can help forgive your debt.

Go to finaid.org (www.finaid.org/loans/forgiveness.phtml) to read more about what you can do to make your debt go away.

Best in Show: Three Great Calculators You Didn't Know You Needed

Figuring out which loan will cost the least isn't the only thing that online calculators can do for you. These calculators from the College Board take things one step further to offer you an idea of the debt your parents can take on, what your parents' loan repayment will be, and what your after-college loan payments will look like.

This calculator will help you figure out what your monthly loan payments will be AFTER you graduate from college. You can use it now to make sure that you're not taking on too much debt.

http://apps.collegeboard.com/fincalc/sla.jsp

The calculator can help parents figure out if they can take on more debt to borrow money for their children's college education.

http://apps.collegeboard.com/fincalc/pardebt.jsp

This calculator can help parents figure out what their repayment schedule will be if they borrow money to pay for their children's education.

http://apps.collegeboard.com/fincalc/parpay.jsp

(*For dependent undergraduate students. Amounts for independent and graduate/professional student are different.)

Loan Name	Interest Rate	Fees	Fixed Rate	Variable Rate	Amount Per Year	
Perkins	5%	none	X		$5,000	
Subsidized Stafford	4.5%	1.5%	X		*$3,500-first year *$4,500-second year *$5,500-third year+	
Unsubsidized Stafford	6.8%	1.5%	X		$5,500 (Yr 1-minus subsidized Stafford) $6,500 (Yr 2-minus subsidized Stafford) $7,500 (Yr 3+-minus subsidized Stafford)	
Parent PLUS	7.9%	3% origination fee	X		Total education costs minus financial aid	
Private (Alternative, State, and Other)	Usually higher than Fed rates	variable		X	Total education costs	

Amount Overall	Based on Financial Need	Gov't Subsidized	Who Offers Loan?	Parent Borrows	Student Borrows
$27,500	X	X	Feds		X
*$23,000	X	X	Feds		X
			Feds		X
			Feds	X	
			Banks, state agencies, colleges, and private foundations		X with parent cosigner

College Applications

> " First and foremost, the college admissions essay is an opportunity for you to connect in an *honest and emotional* way with your reader. This is a reader who has a stack of thousands of essays to pore through. He has seen so many in which the applicant is talking about an internship in which she excelled or a student office in which he made a difference. What that reader is really looking for is some actual truth and feeling. And that kind of truth and feeling can come from almost anywhere in your life.
>
> **—From Alan Gelb's blog (Gelblog: How to Conquer the College Admissions Essay and Make the Most of Your Personal Statement) on September 30, 2010** "

MYTH BUSTERS

Myth: I have to apply to as many colleges as possible so that at least one will accept me.

Truth: Most students apply to six or seven colleges. Applying to more than that is usually a waste of time and money.

It wastes time because getting all the pieces such as letters of recommendation, the application, the essay, and your transcripts ready can take several days even if you're quick.

In addition, most colleges ask for an application fee of from $20 to $60. That can add up if you apply to twenty schools.

Besides, the community college in your district or the state school in a nearby town is fairly likely to admit you even if your grades are not the best.

According to the College Board, you should apply to the following types of schools:

✦ One–two applications to schools you are 90 percent sure will admit you (called safety schools).

✦ Two–four applications to schools you are 75 percent sure will admit you (called probable schools).

✦ One–two applications to schools you are 50 percent sure will admit you (called reach schools).

Talk to your high school counselor about how many colleges to apply to and how to figure out which schools are the best bets for you, your grades, and your parents' pocketbook.

MYTH BUSTERS

Myth: I can use the same essay over and over again for my college applications.

Truth: College admissions standards are getting tougher. Because some students are applying to twenty or more schools, colleges are making their admissions policy trickier so that only students who really want to attend that school will bother to apply.

Many schools are asking for new and different essay topics or asking for two different essays to be sent. For this reason, you probably won't be able to "recycle" one essay over and over again.

—from the College Board

Sample College Essay Questions

How do they come up with those questions? Simple. The college admissions teams at most schools have been reading admissions essays from prospective students for years. Those years of experience help them to craft ever more difficult and telling questions.

Telling? Yes. They want to find out which students really want to attend their school and which students are applying only to have a "safety" school—or three. The types of questions asked by admissions teams fall into three categories as follows:

What would you like to write about?

This type of question lets you choose your own question or includes only the most broad idea for you to narrow down as you will. Actually, this type of question is more difficult because you need to narrow down the broad theme or choose a topic that you can write about in approximately 500 words.

You chose us because . . . ?

This question asks students why they have chosen the school in the first place. The question seems easy at the outset, but it's even trickier than making you choose your own question.

You want to impress the admissions team with your reasons for choosing their school and not repeat what everyone else said. That means that you probably need to do some research about the history of the school and about your major department.

Tell us about yourself.

This type of prompt is common and quite difficult. You want to tell them why you would be a wonderful addition to their campus while also giving some personal information about yourself. If you err by giving too much of one or the other, your essay will be bogged down. Balance is key to making the most of this type of question.

SAVING TIME: USING THE COMMON APPLICATION

A number of colleges have created what is called the "Common Application." This means that all the schools in the group will accept this application in place of their own. However, some schools also want you to submit additional information.

The Common Application can save you time because you can fill it out online at www.commonapp.org, and many colleges will accept this online version. But check with participating schools because some colleges prefer that you mail the application to them.

Schools that accept this application include Yale, Harvard, Princeton, and 411 others.

Best in Show: The Best Websites for Sample College Essays

Here are three websites that include a number of college application essays for you to read. Looking at these essays should give you enough ideas and insight to write a fabulous college entrance essay for yourself.

http://local.quintcareers.com/Sample_College_Application_Essay_1_West_Point_MS-r1326234-West_Point_MS.html

According to QuintCareers.com this sample essay helped the student get accepted at Princeton.

http://collegeapps.about.com/od/essays/a/EssayYouthBoard.htm

If you read only one sample essay, this is the one. The story about Sophie's work on a local board is an excellent example of how to impress the admissions team. You also want to read the critique of the essay for tips about your own work.

www.collegeboard.com/student/apply/essay-skills/9407.html

www.collegeboard.com/student/apply/essay-skills/9408.html

The College Board includes two sample essays on their website along with critiques. It's worth your time to read both essays and the critiques because you'll be better abie to critique your own work.

Application Toolbox: Five Tips for Writing the College Essay

You want to get accepted to the college of your choice, right? To do that, don't treat your application essay like it's schoolwork.

Start early. Ask your favorite English teacher for help. And follow these tips from the College Board:

1. Make your essay narrow and personal.

You only want to cover one topic and cover it well. One error that students make is trying to cover too much ground in their essays.

Instead, stick to one small topic and cover it thoroughly. You are trying to show the admissions team what kind of person you are.

2. Use specific examples.

Use concrete examples that the reader can taste, smell, touch, or hear. Show; don't tell.

Tell a story no matter what you're writing about and pull the reader into your world.

3. Be sincere.

Don't tell the admissions team what they want to hear: blah, blah, blah. Tell them what you think in your own words.

You are trying to share with them a little bit of yourself. That means that you need to be natural and sincere about what you write.

4. Don't use $10 words.

The admissions team isn't going to be impressed by your vocabulary. Don't use long or complicated words when a more common word will do. Use words that you would normally use in an essay for school. Don't look up words in a thesaurus.

5. Proofread. Proofread. Proofread.

The most common error in college application essays is that students finish them at the last minute and don't proofread. Simple typing errors can ruin your chances with the admissions team.

Proof early and often for your college application essay. In fact, ask your favorite English teacher to help you proof your work.

No matter what you decide to write about, start early on your college admission essay. If you wait until the last minute, you may be putting your college career in jeopardy.

Start early. Finish early. And take the time to proofread your work several times before you send it in.

ASK A LIBRARIAN

If you are worried about your college application essay, go to your local library and ask for help.

Your local librarian can put you in touch with excellent reference sources such as Sarah Myers McGinty's *The College Application Essay.* Your librarian can find sample essays for you, books containing sample essay questions from major colleges, and tips to make your writing sparkle.

You can also go online to your library's web page to find resources to help you write a winning essay that will take the admissions team by storm.

A Short Course on Editing Your Application Essay

Editing an applicatiosn essay for college can be a grueling process. You can make it easier on yourself if you follow these four rules.

1. Take a break.

After you've written the first draft, put the essay away and take a break. Go to a movie or out with friends to clear your mind. At the very least, go and do something you enjoy. You will be able to do a better job of editing if you give yourself a break after the writing.

2. Make friends with an English teacher.

Ask your favorite English teacher to help you edit the draft. If you don't have an English teacher that you can ask, ask a friend who is a good writer or someone you trust to help you edit the essay.

One good way to edit is to read the essay aloud to yourself or to a friend. Make sure that your main idea is clear. Check that your supporting points are concrete and vivid. Does it read smoothly aloud? Ask your friends to summarize your main points. If they can't summarize them, you haven't gotten them across.

3. Rewrite

Rework the essay to make sure that your points are clear and concise. Cut out extra words or words that are too fancy. Tell your story directly and with clear, common words. You don't have to stick to one-syllable words, but try for words that you know well and use often.

4. Proofread

The single most common mistake on college application essays is typos. For this reason, you need to proofread your work more than once. Some English teachers advise that you read the essay backwards—reading the word at the end of the sentence, then the next to last word, etc. This helps to make sure that you haven't accidentally left a word out or misspelled something.

COLLEGE APPLICATIONS

Filling out college applications can be time-consuming and just a little scary. However, if you follow the simple steps in this chapter, you will be able to fill out college applications easily and well without too much stress.

You don't have to be a rocket scientist to fill out the forms and get the letters to the college on time. All you have to do is keep an eye on the deadlines and proceed step-by-step to fill in the application, send the documents they request, and await their answer.

Most colleges require a great deal more than just an application form, but this chapter covers all the pieces that you will need to send or e-mail to the school.

College Application Deadlines: Your Senior Year in Review

Sure, it's your senior year in high school, and you want to enjoy it. However, it's also prime time for you to start scoping out potential colleges and applying to them.

How to keep your social life alive while you plan for the future? Easy. Use the handy calendar below to keep track of what is due for your college applications and when you have to send it.

Summer Before Senior Year in High School

+ Make initial campus visits to schools that interest you.
+ If you haven't already taken the SAT or ACT, schedule them now for early in the semester.

September

+ Make an appointment with your high school counselor. Go over your college plans.

✦ Create your final list of the four to eight schools you plan to apply to.

✦ Check to see if any of your schools offer early admissions programs that let you send an application in November.

✦ Find an English teacher or high school counselor who will help you with your application essays.

October

✦ Ask three teachers or other school personnel to write recommendation letters for you to the colleges you apply to. Provide each person with a self-addressed stamped envelope to send to the college.

✦ Begin writing your application essays.

✦ Ask your parents to have their taxes completed early, so they can fill out the FAFSA as close to January 1 as possible.

November

✦ Email or mail any early application packages that you have completed. Before you send them, make copies for your records.

✦ Check with those writing letters of recommendation for you.

✦ If you have taken the ACT or SAT, make sure that your schools will get the results.

December

✦ Talk to the financial aid office of the schools you are applying to. What forms do they need?

✦ Are all your college applications and essays sent out?

January

✦ With your parents, fill out the online FAFSA application using your parents' tax returns.

- Send your first-semester grades to your colleges.

February

- Check with each college to make sure that all your materials have been received.

March

- Wait for early admissions acceptance letters to arrive.

April

- Wait for regular admissions acceptance letters to arrive.
- Choose the school you will attend. Alert other schools that you will not attend.

May

- Send a thank-you note to everyone who helped you apply to college, including those who wrote recommendation letters and your high school counselor.

June

- Graduate with your class.
- Send your second-semester grades to the school that accepted you.

Summer Before College

- Shop for college.
- Choose your first-semester courses.

—based on information from finaid.org, the College Board, and fastweb.com

For Instance: Talk to Your High School Counselor

Kaylee Stanick was overwhelmed. All her friends were applying to colleges, and she didn't know where to start. She didn't know if she even wanted to go to college. She had no idea what to major in, and she felt stupid.

Every one of her girlfriends seemed so sure of themselves and of their college choices. All Kaylee knew is that she didn't want to be too far from home.

Enter Ms. Caufman, Kaylee's high school counselor.

"So many seniors feel as if they should have their whole life planned already," Caufman explains. "That's not necessary. It's okay to go to college to find out what you want to be when you grow up. Everyone has to take Gen Ed classes the first two years anyway. It's a good time to explore."

Ms. Caufman met with Kaylee several times to help her think about what she liked to do and which colleges were good choices for her. By their last meeting, Kaylee had picked out three colleges in her state that offered some programs she was interested in pursuing. Kaylee plans to apply to all three in the next month, and Ms. Caufman is going to write her a letter of recommendation.

"It's okay to be checking things out at college," Kaylee says. "I finally realized that I don't have to know everything right now. Now I can enjoy my time as a senior without worrying so much."

The Application

Most colleges require you to fill out their individual form. However, a few years back a bunch of colleges banded together and agreed to accept one form—the Common Application—in place of their individual forms. Read the box in this chapter about that form to see if your college is a part of the consortium.

Application form Some schools still require you to print out a form and fill it in with pen or typewriter. But these days most schools allow you to apply online.

If your schools allow online application, go for it. It's easier and faster to apply online. One caveat: before you submit your online application, make a copy of it for your files.

Application fee Some colleges have done away with their application fees in the last few years, but others have increased their fees in an attempt to stop students from applying to too many schools.

Before you apply, go to the website of the school and check out the cost to apply. For most schools, the fee is nonrefundable.

Often, those from low-income families can get the fees waived. Call the Admissions office to check on this option.

MYTH BUSTERS

Myth: Once I'm accepted to a college, I don't have to worry about my high school grades.

Truth: Colleges do care about your grades as a high school senior. Many schools will ask for a transcript for your first-semester grades as a senior before they will admit you. In fact, you may be writing the checks for your first-semester classes when the admissions office asks to see a transcript of your second-semester grades in high school.

Most colleges include an "out" clause in their acceptance letter that says that you are accepted to their school so long as you continue to be successful. If your grades drop too much in your senior year, the college can withdraw its offer of acceptance.

High School Transcripts

Colleges usually want official copies of your high school transcripts. This means that the transcripts must be sent directly from your high school to the college in a sealed envelope.

Check in at your high school's counseling office to see what forms need to be filled out and if you need to pay a fee to get your transcripts sent.

When you are accepted by a school, that school will let you know when to send your second-semester transcripts to them.

The Basics: I've been accepted by three schools. Now what?

First, stop to pat yourself on the back for being accepted at more than one school. Celebrate a little with your friends. Then, it's time to make a decision.

Follow the four steps below to narrow your choices down to the one best school for you.

1. Get advice from your family, friends, and high school personnel.

Ask the people you trust about your choices. Talk to them about how they picked their school and how they would go about comparing the three schools.

Don't forget to talk to your high school counselor and your high school teachers. See if they know anyone who attended any of the schools that have accepted you. Try to talk to others who have attended those schools.

2. Compare the schools—apples to apples.

Compare the schools. You can use the College Board's search program to compare the schools or you can use the organizer at the end of this chapter to compare them.

Remember to compare like to like with the colleges. If you check the enrollment at one, check the enrollment at all of the schools. Also, check the student to teacher ratio at all the schools.

Make sure that you know which schools are urban and which are rural. Which ones have the best facilities or the best department for what you want to study?

3. Visit the campus.

If you haven't visited all three campuses already, do so. You might be surprised at how different you will feel about the school once you're standing in it.

How do you feel? Can you see yourself walking from class to class? Do you feel at home there?

4. Alert the schools to your answer.

Now consider all the advice you've been given, your own comparison chart, and how you felt when you visited all three campuses. Use the factual information as well as your own feelings to choose the school you want to attend.

Remember, there is no one school for you. Many schools can be the right one for you, depending on what you are looking for.

Once you've made a decision, send your YES answer back to the school you'll be attending. Then make sure that you send your NO answer to the other two schools.

Do both things quickly because the two schools that you refused will be able to offer admission to another student.

Test Scores

Some time ago, colleges gave admissions tests to potential freshmen. Today, colleges look at your ACT or SAT scores to see if you are ready for college studies.

ACT You can go on the ACT website to have your scores sent to the schools you plan to apply to.

If you haven't taken the ACT, schedule it soon. When you sign up, you can request that the scores be sent to you and all the schools that you've already applied to for admissions.

SAT Go to the SAT website to request that your scores be sent to the colleges you are applying to. You can also request that any other SAT subject tests that you've taken can be sent at the same time.

Check with your schools to see which accept SAT and which accept ACT. Schedule these tests as soon as you can in your senior year so that the scores can be sent to the schools you choose.

Letters of Recommendation

Many colleges require that you get three letters of recommendation from adults who know you, your schoolwork, and your career goals.

The most important point here is to ask people early to write letters for you. You need to give them two to four weeks to write the letter.

Finding the right person Think carefully about which three people to ask. First, make sure that you know how many letters are required for each school you plan to apply to.

In most cases, you can use the same letter to all the schools you wish to attend. However, some schools have forms that need to be filled out rather than letters written. Check with the admissions office of your school to figure out what is required.

You can ask a teacher, your counselor, a minister from your church, or some other adult who knows you well. You can't ask a family member.

Create a list of the three people you'd like to ask and include a second choice for each one in case that person doesn't have time to write a letter for you.

Asking the right person Ideally, you want to choose someone who has wonderful things to say about you. However, if you're not absolutely certain that this person can wholeheartedly confirm what a great person you are, be cautious about how you ask for help.

Approach each person and ask if he or she has time to write a letter of recommendation for you.

If the person says that he or she doesn't have time, thank the person and go to your second choice.

If the person says yes, be prepared with the information from the college (some colleges want letters that address specific subjects such as your schoolwork or your ability to study) and a self-addressed stamped envelope (SASE) for the recommender to send the letter in.

The SASE should already have the address on it where the letter needs to go. Remember to tell the recommender if the letter needs to be on school letterhead or meet any other requirements from your college.

Helping the right person Teachers and other school personnel are frequently asked to write these letters, so most of them know what to do.

If you have asked your employer who probably has less experience with this type of letter, you can offer some facts about you, your extra-curricular activities, and your career goals. This information can help the person write a good letter about you.

After the letter is sent After the letters are written and sent, write a thank-you note to everyone who wrote a letter for you. Don't copy the same text over for each person.

If this person can write a whole letter about you, you can write a few sentences to explain how much you appreciated his or her help with your college application.

Application Essay

Pretty much every college now requires some kind of written explanation or essay in the application packet. Be sure to start yours early, and ask your friends and family for help editing it.

Before you write Brainstorm before you begin writing the essay. You can make a list or ask your friends to help you think of good topics that will showcase what is unique about you.

Look at some sample essays, but don't try to pattern your essay after anyone else's work. It needs to be original.

During the writing Give yourself plenty of time to write the rough draft. Don't do it at the last minute.

Write down everything you can think of that might apply to your topic. You can always take it out later if the piece is too long.

Pay attention to the rules from your school. Some colleges want essays to be a specific word count or page count. Do not send them more or less than they asked for. Sending a longer essay does not mean that they will read all of it.

After the writing Give yourself time to relax after you have written the first draft. Take a little time off. If possible, give yourself at least a week before you try to edit the essay.

Ask for help from your friends who do well in English class or ask an English teacher or other adult to help you edit the essay.

Proof your writing more than once to make sure that you catch any typos.

Interview

Even if you live across the country from the school you want to attend, it can be a good idea to ask for an interview.

With today's technology, you can set up a video interview with the admissions office. If possible, agree to meet with a local alum from that school or go to the school in person to interview.

You want somebody on the admissions team to have met you before the college makes a decision about you.

Artists and Musicians Only

If you plan to study music, acting, dance, art, or design at school, you will probably be asked to schedule an audition or a portfolio review during the application process.

You will have to play or sing or perform something for a committee of faculty members. If you are good enough, they will accept you into their program.

No matter how good your grades are or your other application materials, you won't be able to get into an arts program if your audition or portfolio wasn't what they are looking for.

However, this is an excellent opportunity to bond with some potential faculty members. Be friendly, respectful, and eager to tell them how much you want to attend their school,

Best in Show: The Best Books About Applying to College

Applying to colleges can be difficult and take a great deal of time. You can save yourself much of the worry and work by consulting these two books on the subject.

The Ultimate Scholarship Guide (published every year)

Gen and Kelly Tanabe's book *The Ultimate Scholarship Guide 2011* is much more than just a guide to find scholarships. The Tanabes explain how to get recommendation letters, how to write a good essay, and how to think about your college choices.

It's an excellent resource to own, but it's also a great book to get from the local library if your budget is tight.

The College Application Essay

Sarah Myers McGinty's *The College Application Essay* is a good resource for writing the essay that gains you admittance to your #1

school. McGinty talks about how to choose a topic and how to whittle it down to something you can cover in a short essay. She also explains how to overcome procrastination and writer's block.

You can get it from the library, of course, but it's also an excellent resource for good writing advice.

COLLEGE APPLICATION TRACKING WORKSHEET

	School #1	School #2	School #3
Application Package			
Sent application form Email /mail?			
Application fee			
Safety School? Probable School? Reach School?			
Application deadline			
Fast Track/ Early App deadline			
Transcripts			
Sent first-semester grades			
Sent second-semester grades			
Test Scores			
SAT scores sent			
ACT scores sent			
Misc. scores sent			
Misc. scores sent			

	School #1	School #2	School #3
Letters of Recommendation			
Letter #1			
Person writing it?			
Send thank-you note?			
Letter #2			
Person writing it?			
Send thank-you note?			
Letter #3			
Person writing it?			
Send thank-you note?			
Application Essay			
Date sent e-mail / mail?			
Entrance Interview			
Date scheduled			
Sent thank-you note?			
Audition/Portfolio Review			
Date scheduled			
Financial Aid Forms			
Deadline for filing financial aid forms			
FAFSA sent Online/mail?			

	School #1	School #2	School #3
Special college fin aid form sent?			
Special state aid form sent?			
Results			
Not admitted letter rec'd			
Wait list letter rec'd			
Admitted letter rec'd			
Fin aid letter rec'd			
Deadline to ACCEPT admission			
Deadline to ACCEPT fin aid offer			
NO THANKS sent to other colleges?			

Bibliography/ Webliography

Career Information

Websites

JobStar.org

http://jobstar.org/tools/career/car-lib.php

College Applications

Books

McGinty, Sarah Myers. *The College Application Essay.* (Princeton, NJ: The College Board, 2004.)

Websites

The Common Application

www.commonapp.org

Tracking College Applications

College Board's My Organizer App

https://ecl.collegeboard.com/account/login.jsp?applicationId=0&destinationpage=https%3A%2F%2Fmyorganizer.collegeboard.com%2Fmy_organizer%2FMyOrganizer.jsp

Writing the Application Essay

http://local.quintcareers.com/Sample_College_Application_Essay_1_West_Point_MS-r1326234-West_Point_MS.html

Sample Application Essays

http://collegeapps.about.com/od/essays/a/EssayYouthBoard.htm

www.collegeboard.com/student/apply/essay-skills/9407.html

www.collegeboard.com/student/apply/essay-skills/9408.html

College Costs

Websites

College Cost Calculators

FinAid.org

www.finaid.org/calculators/costprojector.phtml

College Board

http://apps.collegeboard.com/fincalc/college_cost.jsp

The College Savings Plan Network

www.collegesavings.org/collegeCostCalculator.aspx

National Center for Education Statistics

http://nces.ed.gov/fastfacts/display.asp?id=76

Trends in High Education Report

www.collegeboard.com/trends

Financial Aid

Websites

FAFSA Information

www.fafsa.ed.gov

FAFSA Web Worksheet

www.fafsa.ed.gov/before001.htm

Sample Financial Aid Letter

https://studentaid2.ed.gov/getmoney/pay_for_college/award.html

Grants

Websites

Female Student Grants

American Association of University Women

www.aauw.org/learn/fellows_directory/index.cfm

The Educational Foundation for Women in Accounting

www.efwa.org

Finding a Grant

Academic Competitiveness Grant (ACG)

www.studentaid.ed.gov/PORTALSWebApp/students/english/
AcademicGrants.jsp?tab=funding

College Board

http://apps.collegeboard.com/cbsearch_ss/welcome.jsp

Federal Government

www2.ed.gov/fund/grants-college.html?src=fp

The National Science & Mathematics Access to Retain Talent Grant
(National SMART Grant)

www.studentaid.ed.gov/PORTALSWebApp/students/english/Smart-
Grants.jsp?tab=funding

Minority Student Grants

If you are African American, Hispanic, or Native American, you may be
eligible for minority grants. Check out the listings at

FinAid.org:

www.finaid.org/otheraid/minority.phtml

A Better Chance (guide to college resources for students of color)

http://abetterchance.org/abetterchance.aspx?pgID=1087

American Indian College Fund

www.collegefund.org

Hispanic College Fund

www.hispanicfund.org

Indian Affairs

www.bia.gov/index.htm

National Association of Hispanic Nurses
www.thehispanicnurses.org
National Black Nurses Association
www.nbna.org
United Negro College Fund
www.uncf.org/ForStudents/index.asp

Grant Scams
oig.hotline@ed.gov

Writing a Grant Proposal
The Foundation Center online course in proposal writing to win grants:
http://foundationcenter.org/getstarted/tutorials/shortcourse/;jsessionid=J4
PFCCUBKX0PTLAQBQ4CGXD5AAAACI2F

Internships

E-books
The Quintessential Guide to Finding and Maximizing Internships
www.quintcareers.com/Quintessential_Careers_Press/Internship_Guide/

Websites
Finding an Internship
www.interninc.com
www.internweb.com
www.internjobs.com

Jobs

Books
Hiam, Alex, and Susan Angle. *Adventure Careers.* (Clifton Park, NJ: Thomson Delmar Learning, 1995.)

Landes, Michael. *The Back Door Guide to Short-Term Job Adventures: Internships, Extraordinary Experiences, Seasonal Jobs, Volunteering, Work Abroad.* (Berkeley, CA: Ten Speed Press, 2005.)

Websites
California jobs
www.jobstar.org
Camp or national park jobs
www.coolworks.com

www.campstaff.com
www.campjobs.com
www.mysummers.com/default.aspx
College painter jobs
www1.collegepro.com/sb.cn
Cover letters
www.aftercollege.com/content/career_resources/e/cover_letters_an_
endangered_species
www.collegecentral.com/ArticleList.cfm?CatID=CAR
Cruise ship, resort, and camp jobs
www.a+summerjobs.com
www.resortjobs.com
Interviewing
http://college.monster.com/training/articles/2-what-is-monstercollege
http://jobstar.org/index.php
www.worktree.com/index.cfm
www.bls.gov/oco/oc020045.htm
Overseas jobs
www.summer-jobs.com
Summer jobs
www.monster.com
www.snagajob.com
www.getthatgig.com
www.summerjobs.com
Virtual Jobs
www.demandstudios.com
Writing a Résumé
www.ehow.com/first-resume
www.internweb.com/articles

Loans

Websites
Calculators
Loan Comparison Calculator
http://apps.collegeboard.com/loancompare/loancomparison.doc

Student Loan Payment Calculator After Graduation
http://apps.collegeboard.com/fincalc/sla.jsp
Parent Calculator to Take on More Debt
http://apps.collegeboard.com/fincalc/pardebt.jsp
Parent Loan Calculator
http://apps.collegeboard.com/fincalc/parpay.jsp

Loan forgiveness

Public Service Loan Forgiveness (PSLF) http://studentaid.ed.gov/
PORTALSWebApp/students/english/PSF.jsp.
Non–Public Service Loan Forgiveness
www.finaid.org/loans/forgiveness.phtml

Loan repayment

Income-based Repayment
www.ibrinfo.org

Student loan lenders

✦ FinAid.org list of lenders for student loans. www.finaid.org/loans/
educationlenders.phtml
✦ College Board includes student loans in their scholarship search
engine. http://apps.collegeboard.com/cbsearch_ss/welcome.jsp
✦ Military.com has a listing of scholarships, grants, and loans for those
in the military community including veterans, spouses, and children of
soldiers. http://aid.military.com/scholarship/search-for-scholarships.do
✦ Sallie Mae offers student loans along with 529 savings plans. www
.salliemae.com

Tax deductions for loans

Read IRS publication 970 (Tax Benefits for Education) to get all the information at www.irs.gov/publications/p970/index.html.

Paying for College

Websites

529 Savings Plans
www.collegesavings.org/index.aspx
College savings bank cd
www.collegesavings.com

College savings bonds
www.savingsbondsdirect.gov
Federal tax credits
IRS Publication 970, "Tax Benefits for Education"
www.irs.gov
Savings social networking programs
BabyCenter
www.babycenter.com
BabyMint
www.babymint.com
Fidelity 529 College Rewards MasterCard
www.fidelity.com/college
FutureTrust
www.futuretrust.com
MyKidsCollege
www.mykidscollege.com
SAGE Tuition Rewards Program
www.sagescholars.com
Upromise
www.upromise.com

Scholarships

Books

The College Board. *Scholarship Handbook 2011* (published every year). (Princeton, NJ: The College Board, 2010.)

Tanabe, Gen, and Kelly Tanabe. *The Ultimate Scholarship Guide 2011* (published every year). (Belmont, CA: SuperCollege, LLC, 2010.)

Websites
Searching for Scholarships
About Scholarship Search Engines
www.finaid.org/scholarships/awardcount.phtml#matchquality
College Board
http://apps.collegeboard.com/cbsearch_ss/welcome.jsp
College View
www.collegeview.com/financialaid/index.html

FastWeb.com
www.fastweb.com
Federal Government
https://studentaid2.ed.gov/getmoney/scholarship/v3browse.asp
FindTuition.com
www.findtuition.com/scholarships
Military
http://aid.military.com/scholarship/search-for-scholarships.do
Sallie Mae
www.collegeanswer.com/paying/scholarship_search/pay_scholarship_
search.jsp
Scholarly Societies
www.scholarly-societies.org
Scholarships.com
www.scholarships.com
Specific major scholarships
www.finaid.org/otheraid/majors.phtml
State Higher Education Agency Listings
http://wdcrobcolp01.ed.gov/Programs/EROD/org_list.cfm?category_
ID=SHE
Taxes on Scholarships
IRS Publication 970, "Tax Benefits for Education"
http://www.irs.gov
Winning a Scholarship
U.S. Department of Education
http://studentaid.ed.gov/PORTALSWebApp/students/english/scholar-
ships.jsp?tab=funding
College Board
www.collegeboard.com/student/pay/scholarships-and-aid/8937.html
FinAid
www.finaid.org/scholarships/winning.phtml
Volunteering
Websites
Find Volunteer Gigs
www.nps.gov/getinvolved/volunteer.htm
www.serve.gov

Index